Frenchtown

by John Rodabough

Printed in U.S.A
by Christian Board of Publication, St. Louis, Mo.

LIBRARY OF CONGRESS
CATALOG CARD NO.: 80-53306
ISBN 0-86629-021-4

Book design by Tom Alagna

Published by Sunrise Publishing Company, Inc.
10617 Liberty Avenue, St. Louis, Mo. 63132

For Elise --
        a most charming guide.

Contents

Frenchtown

The modern downtown traveller heading south
on Seventh Street notices nothing dramatic after
passing Busch Stadium. A short dip gives way to a
gentle incline, which levels out at Chouteau
Avenue. A few old warehouses stand to the left,
and the world-famous complex of Ralston Purina
dominates the right. Nothing in view indicates that
this ground is in any way special. But, for those rare
few, possessed of a sixth sense, there is immediate
recognition that this is the entry to a special realm,
a realm where ghosts of fabulous men and women
still haunt those who come to seek them. This is the
realm of that lost neighborhood once known as
Frenchtown.

John Rodabough

Sans Souci

Frenchtown, that most romantic of all nineteenth-century St. Louis neighborhoods--Chouteau's Pond to Sugar Loaf Mound. Wainwright's Brewery, Sts. Peter and Paul Church, DeMenil's Mansion, Cracker Castle--they were all a part of that section that gave birth to the modern Soulard and LaSalle Park.

In its day, Frenchtown was the melting pot of the various European ethnic groups and the location of some of the most aristocratic enclaves in the city of St. Louis. Its alleys were the dirtiest, its avenues were the most magnificent, and its charm beguiled all.

Today, the very name FRENCHTOWN has been forgotten by all except a few of the city's oldest inhabitants. The tales of its residents, those tales that can be reconstructed, have the stamp of that from which legends are created.

When Laclede stepped ashore at the limestone bluff which the French were to call "ores du Mississippy," few imagined that the site would eventually become a great city. When the French ceded Louisiana to the United States in 1803, the community was little more than a village. On March 9, 1804, the inhabitants of the town, almost exclusively French, gathered at the southeast corner of First and Walnut streets to witness the event. The tricolor was lowered and up went the Stars and Stripes. A call was made for three cheers for the American flag, but no cheers were given--only tears were evident.

As late as 1818 the town only had two thousand people, and still two-thirds were French.

> The prevailing language of the white persons on the streets was French; The negroes of the town all spoke French. All the inhabitants used French to the negroes, their horses, and their dogs, and used the same tongue in driving their ox-teams.

But, in the years to come, the city became more and more an American city. Only to the south, in a region which the Spanish officials frequently referred to as "The Feliciana" [the happy land], did some of the old way of life survive.

In those early years a small creek, known as "Petite Rivière," served as the southern boundary of St. Louis. A dam and mill trapped its waters, and it became known as Mill Creek. Locals named the resultant pond for the later owner, Auguste Chouteau. The road to Carondelet, known in the nineteenth century by the village of its destination, ran close to the Mississippi River. A later course

9

Chouteau's Pond. The two large structures in the background are McDowell's medical buildings.

shift moved the river to the east. A dense growth of trees stretched from Chouteau's Pond to the present Arsenal Street, then the location of a village housing the remnants of the Delaware and Shawnee tribes, now united as one. A reminder of even earlier Indian habitation was, and is, Sugar Loaf Mound, just east of the present intersection of U. S. Highway 55 and Broadway--the last remaining of the earthenworks which once gave to this metropolis the nickname of "Mound City."

Crowded between the Carondelet Road and the river, and stretching from Chouteau's Pond south to Sugar Loaf, was a row of what were mansions in that day. These estates, mostly used by city merchants as country residences, were the beginning of Frenchtown. The northern-most of these properties was that of Gabriel Cerré, a man whose descendants would be related to the Chouteaus, Pauls, Vallés, Billons, Hams, DeMenils, Gareschés, Papins, Gratiots, Provencheres, and many others, the elite of the French families of St. Louis. These families formed the nucleus of the French community south of St. Louis. In speaking of these people, one early settler wrote:

They were, beyond doubt, the most happy and contented people that ever lived. They believed in enjoying life. There was a fiddle in every house, and a dance somewhere every night. They were honest, hospitable, confiding, and generous. No man locked his door at night, and the inhabitant slept in security, and soundly, giving himself no concern for the safety of

10

the horse in his stable or
of the household goods
and effects in his habitation.

Gabriel Cerré, a Canadian by birth, was a merchant at Kaskaskia, Illinois, for twenty-five years before moving to St. Louis in 1780. When he arrived in the community, it was a bustling center of fur trade, and Indians were frequently seen on the streets. For the next twenty-five years Cerré was a major figure participating in the commerce of St. Louis. Through the winter and spring months, when trade flourished, Cerré remained in town. But as soon as the hot languid summers arrived, he departed for his summer house just southeast of the present Park and Broadway. There beckoned the easy life. That limestone dwelling, with its wide galleries, set amidst the most famous orchards in this area, was a most comfortable retreat. As poets are wont to say:

In that mansion used to be
Free-hearted hospitality.

It was just as well that the polished floors of Cerré's mansion had no carpets, for frequent were the occasions when the violin came out, and the music swelled to the accompaniment of various quadrilles and minuets. Powdered wigs and rare silks were donned, and European elegance played out a tableau against a frontier backdrop. During such an occasion Cerré demonstrated that business and pleasure could truly go hand in hand by announcing the marriage of his daughter, Marie Therese, to Auguste Chouteau, and at a later date, Julia to Antoine Pierre Soulard. By these two alliances Cerré truly guaranteed his descendants the first rank in the wealth and society of St. Louis.

In the coming generation the Soulards and Chouteaus would be the most envied of an envied group--the French aristocracy of St. Louis. True,

there was to be an American aristocracy in the city, and a Negro aristocracy as well, and later, even a German aristocracy, but the French aristocracy-- well, everyone who mattered knew there was no other that mattered. After all, "Crème de lâ Crème" has no equivalent in anyone else's language.

Gabriel Cerré

When Cerré died April 4, 1805, he left his country estate to Julia and Antoine Soulard, who were to make this their home throughout their married life. Julia Cerré landed a prize catch in Soulard. Born in France in 1766, he joined the French military, and then fled the country during the revolution, arriving in St. Louis in 1794. He was appointed surveyor for Upper Louisiana, a post he held until the French ceded the lands to the United States. In payment for his duties as surveyor, he was granted 122 acres stretching southwest from the inter- section of Park and Carondelet Road. This, added to the Cerré inheritance, constituted the Soulard tract which would become fantastically valuable when the city eventually spread southward.

11

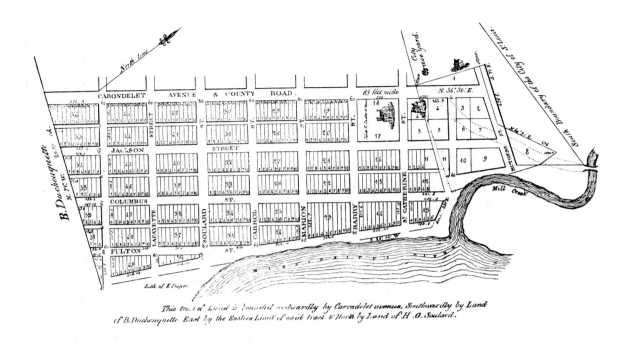

SOULARD'S ADDITION TO ST. LOUIS.

After the United States acquired Louisiana, Soulard retired to his orchards and lived the life of a gentleman farmer. He and his wife continued the Cerré tradition of gracious entertaining, with guests frequently under their roof. That Soulard had a devilish sense of humor is demonstrated by one who remembered the old gentleman saying:

> "Blessed are those who have children,"...Then, as the proud parents smiled and bowed acquiescence, he added, "But twice blessed are those who have none."

Antoine Soulard died November 9, 1825. For a number of years, his widow lived quietly in the old home. Then, with St. Louis beginning to grow her way, she saw the possibilities of acquiring great wealth. In 1836 she began selling her acreage at Carondelet Road and Park. With the proceeds she built the next year a twenty-room brick mansion set in an entire block. The yard was a carpet of wild violets. From its hill site she had a commanding view of the river.

June 21, 1838, Mrs. Soulard set aside two city blocks to be used for a public market. This was the beginning of the establishment which still bears her name. The early years of the market were truly humble as it was quite removed from the population of the city and had stiff competition from the much larger and better located Convent, or French, Market at Chouteau and Broadway. The unusual name for the latter market resulted from its nearby neighbor, Sacred Heart Convent, a local landmark until its removal in 1890. The name FRENCH MARKET was used well into the twentieth century to designate the South Broadway shopping area. There were other markets in the nearby area, but today Soulard stands unchallenged--the heir to over two centuries of public marketing in St. Louis.

In 1844 the Soulard mansion was sold to the Catholic Church, and a magnificent structure, St. Vincent de Paul, was begun immediately to its

12

Julia Soulard's mansion.

north. That structure was consecrated November 5, 1845. Mrs. Soulard did not live to see this, as she died May 9, 1845. In later years the Soulard mansion was divided into two houses and eventually demolished in February, 1952. Highway 55 now runs over the site.

Antoine and Julia Soulard's son, Henry Gustave, resided on a farm at the junction of the Mississippi and Missouri Rivers until 1839. He and his wife then moved to part of the Soulard property in the city and built a beautiful Greek Revival mansion on the entire block southwest of the intersection of Hamtramck (named for Mrs. Henry Soulard's grandfather, a famous figure of the Revolutionary War, and recently rechristened as Tucker Boulevard) and Soulard. This dwelling, with its great gilt mirrors, pictured walls, and famed library, was one of the great mansions of its day. The gala balls held there were legendary. Henry Soulard died in the house on February 16, 1891. The house did not long survive him. It was badly damaged in the tornado of May 31, 1896, and had to be removed. The same tornado levelled the old Soulard market buildings.

Another of Antoine Soulard's sons prominent in St. Louis affairs was Benjamin Antoine, who "never lived long at any address." His time was absorbed by real estate transactions. He was forever dealing in subdivisions, selling off the Soulard lands and acquiring great wealth. Mr. Soulard might personally have felt nothing but disdain for the Americans and Germans flocking into St. Louis, but he showed little hesitancy in garnering in their dollars. In a few years he changed the southern end of Frenchtown into a German city!

However, he considered his crowning achievement to be the marriage of his daughter, Rose Mary, to Capt. Nicholas C. Washington, a descendant of the family of President George Washington. This union was one of the most talked-about weddings in the nineteenth-century St. Louis, the marriage of a member of a first family of St. Louis to a member of the first family of the nation! The site of the gala affair was the grand Church of the Annunciation at Sixth and Labadie. The wedding was held January 31, 1866. A magnificent ball followed, attended by the "beauty and fashion of the city." This marriage was a sensation, but the following year Mrs. Rose Mary Washington created an even greater sensation by bringing suit for a divorce. A Catholic divorce involving a first family of the French community! Alas--it had to be the American influence!

Today the Soulard name has come to be applied to the large area south of the old mansions and market. Much of South St. Louis has thus come to be their monument.

Gabriel Cerré's other daughter, Marie Thérèse Cerré, married Auguste Chouteau on September 21, 1786. He was one of the founders of St. Louis and was its wealthiest citizen in those early years. He built his mansion in the city but was never to live in Frenchtown. However, many of his descendants chose that area for their homes.

13

Soulard Market Building. This is the only known photograph of this historic building. It was taken just before the tornado of 1896.

The Chouteau and Soulard names are better known today, but in the nineteenth century no family was more famous than their relatives, the Pauls. Eustache Paul, the founder of the family, had been an admiral in the French navy. He had retired to a huge sugar plantation on San Domingo and lived there for a number of years, sending his children back to Paris to be educated.

When the drums began to beat and unrest spread among the tens of thousands of slaves on the island, Eustache sent his wife, Marie Anne Scholastique Mace, to France and safety. When blood was flowing down the streets of Port au Prince, Eustache fled to a ship sailing for Europe. But, he was too late. Already he had been poisoned by one of his slaves. He died aboard ship and was buried at sea.

The widow Paul and her four children remained in France for several years. Her son, Louis René Paul, born in Cape Francois, San Domingo, in 1783, was educated in Paris at the Ecole Polytechnique. He served in the French navy and was badly wounded in the Battle of Trafalgar. As a former Colonel of Engineers under Napoleon, he was welcomed when he arrived in the United States in 1808. Within a year he had made his way to St. Louis.

Paul, the most sophisticated young man in St. Louis, dazzled the local society. A man of many social accomplishments, he introduced the waltz to the city. Had he possessed no other skill, that contribution, in a culture so devoted to the goddess

14

(*Above*) Broadway in August, 1845. The view is to the south. The building in the center is the French Market. It stood at the corner of Chouteau Avenue.
(*Below*) Customers doing their marketing.

Henry Gustave Soulard's mansion. Its landscaped grounds covered an entire block.

of dance, would have established him in the forefront of local society. From 1809 to 1813, he conducted business in partnership with Bartholomew Berthold. Paul then engaged in surveying government lands. In his travels he often came in contact with various Indian nations. Adept at languages, he soon acquired a thorough knowledge of their various tongues. In later years he would often be called upon to serve as interpreter in matters involving St. Louis businessmen and Indians.

In 1817 René's brother, Gabriel Rival Paul, joined him in St. Louis. The next year the brother married Marie Louisa, the daughter of Colonel Auguste

René Paul

Tullia Paul Beckwith's pleasure cottage. This structure, on Seventh Street, was the center of St. Louis social life in the 1840's and 1850's. It was torn down in the summer of 1978.

Chouteau. Not to be outdone, René Paul also married a daughter of Colonel Chouteau, the beautiful Eulalie. He died May 20, 1851. Several of his children, Edmund W., Amelia, and Tullia Clementia, were to be intimately associated with Frenchtown. Tullia was the first and most important of the family to settle in the area.

From her mother Tullia inherited property south of Chouteau Avenue along Seventh Street. There, she constructed a mansion in 1841, probably designed by her uncle, Gabriel Paul, St. Louis' first architect. On May 5, 1842, Tullia married Frederick Williams Beckwith, a recent arrival from Kentucky. Because of throat trouble he had given up the

ministry to go into business. Tullia, the reigning queen of St. Louis society, was beautiful, gay, and carefree. She entertained lavishly. The acres of ground around her mansion were beautifully landscaped, and she often filled them with outdoor concerts, dances, and masquerades. On these occasions, the music was divine. Only the finest German orchestras were employed. The single violin of the old days had been forgotten. The French danced through the night to the strains of German music. It is said that Tullia Paul spent more than one fortune giving pleasure to others. "Entrée to her house was the goal for which all aspirants to social position fondly hoped." If ever a name would

17

have been needed for the Beckwith household, Sans Souci would have sufficed.

Frederick Beckwith died in 1854. Tullia then sold much of the property surrounding her house for a sub-division. This property, much of which was ideally suited for business purposes, brought proceeds amounting to a handsome fortune, one of the several she spent entertaining her friends. Tullia then leased her mansion and travelled extensively in Europe. Streets in her subdivision carried family names--Ham (now Ninth), Amelia (now Lebanon), Paul (now vanished).

Tullia's daughter, Minerva, was the most beautiful belle of old St. Louis. Her presence was all that was necessary to guarantee the success of any occasion. Minerva loved to travel and had engraved on her visiting cards a butterfly with the motto, "On the wing."

> Those who were young in those days before the war and change and death broke up that happy household remember how it was the centre of all that was gay and bright in the social life of St. Louis for years... No people ever enjoyed the ease, refinement, and luxury which wealth brings in a more liberal and generous fashion.

But, then the tragedies began. Shortly after her marriage to William Hull, the beautiful Minerva died. Tullia ran afoul of the United States army during the divisive years of the Civil War and lost much of her fortune. Never one to watch pennies, Tullia in her later years found herself penniless. Like Scarlett, she never worried. She turned to her talent for music and languages, walking the streets of St. Louis, giving lessons on the guitar and the piano, and teaching her beloved French language. To the end she was the personification of charm and grace and was admired by all. She died July 15, 1898. It then seemed as if the locusts descended upon St. Louis society.

As previously mentioned, the French of St. Louis were clannish and tended to socialize only among themselves, and often within family circles. The small community necessitated frequent marriage between cousins, making relationships complex. Within their circle the French spoke only their native language. They had a tendency to ignore their newer English-and-German-speaking neighbors. Among their clannish organizations was the French Benevolent Society whose banquets were restricted to those of French nationality. From January 7, 1854, to October 6, 1865, St. Louis had its own French language newspaper, *Le Revue De L'Ouest*, a weekly journal which eventually failed for lack of financial support. The French community had become too small to support business ventures which smacked of separatism. By then it had become apparent that French culture could only flourish in the drawing room. Old families who visited over gumbo dinners reminisced late into the night. For many the past remained not as a memory, but as more real than their present surroundings. For them fifty years before seemed as only yesterday.

When it came to remembrances, none were grander or told with more charm than those of Sophie Chouteau. Although her niece, Tullia Paul, was the Queen of St. Louis Society, Mrs. Chouteau was the acknowledged matriarch of the town. Born Sophie Labadie, she had married Auguste Pierre Chouteau, the nephew of St. Louis' founder. In the late 1840's the Widow Chouteau moved into her enormous mansion on the south side of Gratiot between Eighth and Ninth streets. The house looked out over the Chouteau Mill Pond, then a splendid sheet of water almost two miles long. There she held court with her beautiful daughter,

Sophie Labadie Chouteau's mansion on Gratiot just west of Eighth Street. The beautiful residence faced east, and had a splendid view of the Mississippi River and Chouteau's Pond.

The parlor in Sophie Labadie Chouteau's mansion. The frescoes, plaster ornamentation, and other decor were as elaborate as any in St. Louis Frenchtown.

Augustine. The parlor of the house was the most lavishly decorated in St. Louis. The talk was that it was gaudy, such poor taste, quite overdone, but secretly all wished it was theirs. Not to be outdone, Augustine's sister, Mrs. Nicholas DeMenil, erected a lavish mansion which still stands at the south end of Frenchtown. It is evidence of the wealth and splendid lifestyle enjoyed by this favored class. In the mid-1850's Mrs. Chouteau moved around the corner to a beautiful mansion on Eighth Street.

When Mrs. Chouteau died during the Civil War, a funeral of a princely scale was conducted for her at the Old Cathedral. Slaves of the various old French families carried her body from the Cathedral. She was the last of the old order. With her perished those who had known St. Louis from its infancy. Many in the crowd sensed that things would never be the same again.

First it was those Americans, then those hopeless Germans, and now the war. Would it never end? Change, change, change! So many changes, and for what? The charm, the quiet graceful life, what had happened to it? The language was disappearing. People could no longer properly pronounce the street names. Where would it all end?

Nicholas DeMenil's country mansion, finished in 1863.

Act of Legislature, Feb. 15th, 1841.

A Bevy Of Nabobs

Lola Montez danced her scandalous spider dance, and Madame English clipped the gullible on the levee. Sweet young things, attempting to pass each other in hoop skirts, squared off to see who would have to get off the walk and navigate the mud of the streets. Young Americas (as the delinquents of the era were known) shouted, kicked, stomped, spat, and in general made life hell for the theater goers. The Courthouse in St. Louis was still abuilding, and many wondered if it would ever be finished. Gas lights were in use, but running water wouldn't come for a few more years. Bricklayers were striking for $2.50 per day, saying $2.00 just wouldn't "put the bacon on the table." The Commercial Baseball Club, that local pioneer, hosted its games at Ham (now Ninth) and Hickory streets--one memorable game resulting in a score of forty-seven to fourteen. The Americans pushed and shoved, they cursed in the streets, and they spoke to outright strangers. It was all so bewildering to the old French families--nothing made sense anymore. What had happened to their quaint city of just a decade before?

St. Louis was growing by leaps and bounds. Americans were pushing west in record droves. The Germans and Irish were starting to come in.

Everyone knew that in a couple of decades the city would rank first in population and seize the capital from the East Coast. Yes, it was a glorious era, the 1850's, and St. Louis was enjoying it to the utmost.

In this mid-nineteenth-century St. Louis lived the greatest collection of millionaires in the Mississippi Valley. Real estate, railroads, and western trade were the basis of their fortunes--fortunes so large that the working classes regarded these men as princes, or better yet, as nabobs. They lived as lavishly as the autocrats of Natchez, and their lifestyle was as dramatic and as romantic as any of the legends for which New Orleans is today famous.

The wealthiest of these men--William Russell, Daniel D. Page, Joshua Brant, Andrew Christy, and James Harrison--were Americans, and they lived in Frenchtown. The western end of Morrison Avenue, Eighth Street between Chouteau and Gratiot, and Chouteau west of Eighth Street, housed collections of these and other famous families. Though their contemporary French and German neighbors are better known today, it was these Americans who set the tone for the lifestyle in nineteenth-century St. Louis.

It did not happen overnight, this American domination of St. Louis. These descendants of settlers of the Eastern Seaboard and the South gradually drifted into the city over a period of decades. Their entrance into the area was not as dramatic as that of the earlier French, or the later Germans, Irish, and that myriad of other ethnic groups that at one time or another settled in Frenchtown, But, in the long run, they outnumbered and absorbed all the others. The resultant blend of cultures was one of the richest, brashest, and most generous societies in the United States, if not the most refined. Mrs. Basil Hall, upon eating at a St. Louis tavern in 1828 wrote:

> An American breakfast or dinner never fails to remind me of the directions given of old for the eating of the passover, "With your loins girded, your shoes on your feet, and your staff in your hand; and ye shall eat it in haste"; and truly if the Israelites obeyed the command with a strictness equalling American speed it must have been a strange scene.

William Russell

In 1804 St. Louis was a small village crowded close to the Mississippi River. Its population was almost exclusively French, and would remain so for many years. A few Americans saw promise in the area and decided to make it their home. One of these was William Russell, destined to become one of the wealthiest and most influential men in the Mississippi Valley.

Russell, a native of Virginia, left his home in Hawkins County, Tennessee, and went north to Cincinnati. He then travelled down the Ohio River, visiting at Louisville and Vincennes. He reached Kaskaskia in November, 1803, and soon came up to Cahokia, but ice flows prevented him from crossing

to St. Louis until February 8, 1804. After a few days in the town, he decided to settle there.

St. Louis then had nine hundred inhabitants. Mail service, when on schedule, was available once a month at Cahokia. The only ferry consisted of two piroques tied together and overlaid with planks. The ferry operator, Calvin Adams, also kept a small tavern. One of the few other Americans in the community was William Sullivan, a former sergeant in the command of Captain Amos Stoddard; he kept a boarding house. The only American store was that of Comegys & Fortune on Main Street. A few Americans were settled at Bonhomme, about five miles above St. Charles on the south bluffs of the Missouri River. This was the American community. All else was French.

Russell had about five hundred dollars with which to make his fortune, and he wasn't at all sure what he wanted to do. There were not many farms near St. Louis, so he tried to be a farmer. He failed. Next he turned to merchandizing. He loaded several flatboats with corn and set out for New Orleans. One of the boats sank, and he lost money on the trip. Later he was fond of saying, "Thus was one merchant spoiled." He then turned to the profession that was to make his fortune--land speculation.

Spain had been exceedingly generous in granting land to its citizens in Louisiana. Those holding such grants were anxious to have them confirmed by the new government of the United States. In stepped William Russell. Russell was employed by the United States as a Deputy Surveyor. His new job took him throughout the wilds of Missouri and Arkansas. He was forever travelling. His services were sought by large numbers, and it is probable that none other presented as many private claims before the Boards of Commissioners as he did. As a result of all the land deals in which he was involved, Mr. Russell became one of the largest land owners in Missouri and Arkansas. He laid out Little Rock, Helena, and several other towns in Arkansas. At that time the plotted town of Little Rock had a challenger, Cadron, in its struggle to become the state capital. Following is a story which shows Russell's ability to manipulate affairs to suit his needs:

> Certain St. Louis speculators laid off the town of Little Rock and got the lone settler made postmaster. Although Little Rock was right in the woods, with only two shacks, when the vote was taken in the legislature, the senate was for Little Rock, and the lower house for Cadron. Then the legislature recessed, and during this time the speaker of the house and certain other well-known politicians bought for nominal sums land on the Little Rock townsite. When the legislature reconvened, the members of the house saw the light, did an about-face, and voted to locate the capitol at Little Rock.

Russell made a fortune by selling a few lots cheap. He used similar tactics many times. Russell was also the father of Alton, Illinois, a town he developed and invested in heavily. He owned much of what is now South St. Louis, and it was on part of these lands that he finally made his home.

South of the Soulards, Russell bought seventy-six acres in 1837, naming it "Crystal Springs Farm." In 1842 he built a fine stone mansion of the Doric order. The house faced east and had an unobstructed view of the Mississippi River. This he presented as a gift to his only child, Ann, newly married to Thomas Allen. Russell and the Allens lived together in this country setting, close to the city, and yet remote from the noise and pollution.

In his later years William Russell was determined to put his affairs in order and make peace with everyone. He had earlier encouraged his brothers, James and Joseph, to settle in St. Louis. As they were poor, he gave them lands and established them among the country gentry of the area.

James Russell's 432-acre estate, known as "Oak Hill," was immediately south of Henry Shaw's "Tower Grove." Shaw once asked him to cut down the trees which surrounded his house; it seemed they were obstructing Mr. Shaw's view of the river. This ended their friendship. Coal, discovered at "Oak Hill," became a major source of income for James. William Russell further supplemented James' income by educating his brother's children and giving them lands and money. This he did for all his other nephews and nieces, a considerable undertaking as they numbered over thirty people. A grandson of James Russell was the famous artist of the American West, Charles M. Russell.

In December, 1854, William Russell suffered a stroke which left his right side paralyzed. He was thereafter confined to his room. Russell set about preparing for death with the same attention to detail that had made him one of the greatest businessmen of St. Louis. He erected his own tomb in Bellefontaine Cemetery. Never having had time for religion, he now found that time. He hired his own chaplain, who daily administered to him. In September, 1856, he joined the Presbyterian Church. Thereafter, reading and talking hourly with his chaplain, he was ready for death. The fateful event occurred July 14, 1857. He was eighty years, one month, and eleven days.

Though his fortune had amounted to millions of dollars, he had passed it all ahead of time to his daughter and relatives. He owned nothing when he died. There was no need for a probate. His grave awaited. Everything had been taken care of. William Russell was surely an orderly man.

William Russell's Doric mansion. The photograph was taken in the 1890's.

When Thomas Allen moved to St. Louis in the spring of 1842, he found Miss Ann C. Russell to be "quite the belle of the town." He courted her and swept her off her feet. On July 12, 1842, they were married. With the aid of her enormous fortune, Allen was to quickly become one of the leaders in the St. Louis business community.

Thomas Allen was born at Pittsfield, Massachusetts, August 29, 1813. He was a graduate of Union College and studied law at Albany, New York. In 1837 he began publication of a newspaper, *The Madisonian*, in Washington, D. C. He was an intimate associate of General William Henry Harrison, and would have enjoyed great influence during his presidency, had it not been ended so abruptly by Harrison's death. Allen opened a law office in St. Louis, but did not long pursue that profession. In 1848 he met his destiny, when he made an address on behalf of the St. Louis and Cincinnati Railroad. From that date, he was a leader in the promotion of railroad development.

In 1849 St. Louis turned its attention to the building of a railroad to the Pacific Coast. Allen was the leading spokesman for this railroad, and in 1851 was elected its first president. After the project was well under way, Allen resigned in 1854. In 1867 Allen purchased the Iron Mountain Railroad and greatly extended the line. By 1874 he was president of four railroads. These he consolidated under the title of the St. Louis, Iron Mountain and Southern

Tho. Allen

27

Railway Company, comprising 686 miles of track. Estimates are that this railroad supplied St. Louis $100,000,000 annual trade. In 1880 he sold his interest for $2,000,000 cash. Allen was also active in banking and rebuilt the Southern Hotel after the 1877 fire. That splendid building cost over $1,000,000.

In 1848 Allen had begun to subdivide the ninety acres surrounding "Crystal Springs Farm." Ann, Russell, and Allen streets were projected through the tract. The fine old mansion was left occupying the block northwest of the intersection of Ninth and Russell.

Crystal Springs Farm

In 1862 Allen leased the grounds west of the mansion to William Stumpf and Herman Bachmann, brewers. They operated a picnic grounds and beer garden, known as Union Park. Trees provided shade, and everywhere bloomed beautiful gardens of flowers. From May until October, there were concerts by the best of the German bands-- Waldauer's, Vogel's, Sauter's, etc. In 1866 the Allens moved from "Crystal Springs Farm" to the Planter's Hotel. They later rented the Joshua Brant mansion on Chouteau. In 1870 they moved to a beautiful mansion on Lucas Place.

After a splendid business career Allen was elected as a Democrat to Congress in 1880. Earlier he had failed in attempts to gain national office. His health rapidly failed, and he died at Washington, April 8, 1882. The Allen family then moved to Europe. Thomas Allen's granddaughter, Ann Russell Allen, married Count Paul Festetics, jun de Tolna, of Hungary, in 1899. After their Paris wedding they made their home at the Castle of Mierola, within a few hours of Vienna. They lived the life of le grand monde, often associating with their close friend, the Prince of Wales.

The popularity of Union Park declined, and "Crystal Springs Farm" fell on bad times. It became a foundling home, and in 1896 was badly damaged by the great tornado. Later it was used by the Salvation Army, and then abandoned. Empty for many years, the then dilapidated mansion was torn down in 1921. Gazing upon the dismal site today, it is difficult to imagine the gaiety and the beauty of that bygone era.

Daniel D. Page

That Saturday morning of January 13, 1855, panic swept St. Louis. Page & Bacon, the leading banking house of all the Mississippi Valley, failed to open for business. People rushed to rival banks and withdrew their holdings. Everywhere, talk was of a depression. Fortunes wavered, and some collapsed that fateful day--truly one of the darkest days in the history of St. Louis finance.

How could it have happened? Sure, other banks occasionally failed, but this was Page & Bacon! Page & Bacon, the bank that had the year before handled transactions in excess of $80,000,000! Page

& Bacon, known to have net assets in excess of $3,000,000! Page & Bacon, the usual savior of the financially troubled! Page & Bacon, the bedrock of the financial community of St. Louis! If such a firm as this could fall, what would happen to the less mighty! Cassandras abounded. Pessimism prevailed. Few, wondering what the next day would bring, slept peacefully that night.

Daniel D. Page was born into a wealthy farming family at Parsonsfield, York County, Maine, March 5, 1790. By the time he had reached fifteen, Daniel's family had lost much of its wealth, and the lad had to go to Portland for employment. In a general store there, he learned to be a baker. Later, he went to Boston, and was very successful in that line.

Young Daniel married Deborah Young, and decided to move west. They went by wagon to Pittsburgh, there purchasing a flatboat. They then went downriver to Louisville, there buying produce from the surrounding country. Continuing downriver, they sold and traded their goods along the way. At New Orleans, Daniel entered the tobacco trade and became quite successful. Due to the failing health of his wife, he liquidated his business and prepared to move. The couple purchased grocery goods, loaded them on a boat, and set out for St. Louis. The boat sank, and his supplies were badly damaged, but Page and his wife escaped unharmed.

Daniel and Deborah Page arrived in St. Louis in 1818, immediately opening a grocery business, and later adding a bakery. Their business and residence were located on the east side of Main Street south of Walnut. Page used a two-wheeled delivery wagon, with an oval top and openings on each side. As he drove along, he rang a bell to attract customers to his wares.

Quite early Page acquired a reputation for strict honesty and "upright principles." He thus came to the attention of John Mullanphy, the first person of St. Louis to possess great wealth. Mullanphy quietly visited Page and gave him three or four hundred dollars. His instructions were to use this gift to distribute free bread to the needy. He was never to reveal the source of the money. All the gifts were made as if they were from Page himself. When the fund was depleted, Mullanphy replenished it. "The news soon spread abroad that Page was giving bread to all the poor people down town, and Mr. Page's name and praise was in the mouth of everyone."

By 1829 Page had captured the hearts of all St. Louisans. He was elected, almost unanimously, on a citizen's ticket, as the second Mayor of St. Louis. In that office he created a waterworks, greatly improved the streets, and fathered the local licensing of dogs. In the fall of 1832, he resigned his office, an action "much regretted by all." One contemporary remarked, "Were I a Pliny, I would write a panegyric in favor of D. D. Page."

In 1833 Page built and began operation of the first steam flouring mill of St. Louis, located at the site later known as 22 South First Street. Very little wheat was then grown in the Midwest. To stimulate its production, Page offered "three-times the going rate" for all the grain that could be delivered to him for a year. Wheat suddenly became a very popular crop. Page's mill flourished and grew to giant proportions. By the 1840's Page was a very wealthy man, investing heavily in local real estate. He was also President of the Farmers' and Mechanics' Insurance Company. However, his rise had only begun.

On May 2, 1844, Page's daughter, Julia Ann, married Henry D. Bacon. Of him it was later said:

> There are some men whose characters are so nobly planned by nature, and so plentifully adorned

with those virtues which ennoble humanity, that it is a duty and a pleasure to write their biographies and hand them as memorials to posterity for its benefit and instruction.

Born in East Granville, Massachusetts, May 3, 1818, he had come to St. Louis in 1835 and entered the dry goods business. Later, Bacon served as a river captain, and was noted for his piety. His boat, the Hannibal, always tied up at midnight on Saturday, and remained so until the same hour Sunday night. Still later, he went into the iron trade. After marrying Julia Page, Bacon joined his father-in-law in the flour business.

Henry D. Bacon

In 1848 the banking house of Page & Bacon was organized, located at the southeast corner of Main and Vine streets. Because of Page's vast real estate holdings and the recognized ability and personality of Bacon, this bank rapidly gained the confidence of the people. Then, during the Mexican War, many of the supplies for the soldiers of the United States were purchased in St. Louis. Much of this government money was channeled through the bank of Page & Bacon, rapidly increasing its credit and prestige throughout the West. In 1850 a branch was established in San Francisco. The business done by the bank in 1854 amounted to over $80,000,000. It was the largest bank in the western United States.

Page & Bacon saw that the future of St. Louis would depend on railroad connections, and took the lead in constructing various lines into the city. Page was one of the incorporators of the Pacific Railway Company, now known as the Missouri Pacific. His bank pledged $135,000 toward the construction of that road. The bank also built the Belleville & St. Louis Railroad, bringing cheap coal to the city. But by far the most ambitious of their railroad ventures was the construction of the Mississippi & Ohio Railroad from St. Louis to Vincennes, Indiana. That line was designed to bring the rich trade of all Southern Illinois to St. Louis. Page & Bacon, the exclusive developers of the Mississippi & Ohio, invested $1,250,000, in that enterprise.

Page & Bacon speculated extensively in real estate, building hundreds of moderately-priced dwellings in St. Louis. These they sold on low payments to the German immigrants flooding into the city. The bank also held over $1,000,000 in choice riverfront properties. At the St. Louis Recorder of Deeds Office, Daniel D. Page recorded nearly one thousand real estate transactions.

Page and Bacon became renowned in the realm of philanthropy. Bacon supplied the financial support for the creation of the Mercantile Library, one of the great bulwarks of culture in nineteenth-century St. Louis. He built the Union Presbyterian Church on Locust Street, at a cost of $70,000; he then donated $40,000 toward that cost. St. Louis considered itself lucky to have such wealthy and generous citizens.

Page and Bacon lived on a princely scale. In 1847 Bacon built an enormous mansion on the southeast corner of Morrison and Morton (now Thirteenth Street). His two-acre yard stretched back to Park Avenue. In 1852 Page built an even larger house on a four-acre plot immediately east of that of Bacon. To the east of these households, Page owned a beautiful meadow bounded by Hickory, Eighth, Park, and Eleventh streets. All around his lands were thickly settled neighborhoods. Thus, Page and Bacon lived in their own private park in the midst of a teeming city. So stood the fortunes of this family empire at the beginning of 1855. No one was wealthier in St. Louis. No one was more generous. No one lived on a grander scale. None was more exalted than Page and Bacon.

In 1854 a severe recession swept across the United States. Trade languished, and money became scarce. Building the Mississippi & Ohio Railroad had drawn an immense capital from the

firm. The deposits of Page & Bacon dropped from $1,700,000 to $700,000. The bank was dangerously overextended. Bacon went to New York City and met with the directors of the house of Duncan, Sherman & Company. He was assured that they would extend credit to the St. Louis bank to the amount of $250,000, this backed by real estate securities Bacon had taken with him to New York.

Confident that the bank was secure, Bacon returned to St. Louis. A few days later he received a telegram stating that the line of credit had been withdrawn. Bacon appealed: "For God's sake, do not desert us, if you do we are ruined and half of St. Louis with us." The New York bank refused to honor its commitment. Page & Bacon had to close its doors.

That January 13, 1855, people rushed to all the other banks of St. Louis and began withdrawing their money. By the end of the day, the deposits in the city amounted to $800,000 less than they had in the morning. Providentially, Sunday was at hand. The next day ten of the wealthiest citizens of St. Louis, including James Harrison, Andrew Christy, and Joshua B. Brant--of Frenchtown, pledged their personal fortunes, in excess of $8,000,000, to secure the banks of the city. The panic eased, and there was no run on the banks on Monday.

Page and Bacon were finished as bankers. For a short time there was stagnation of all business in the city--so heavily were local firms dependent on that house. Page, thereafter, retired from active business, and "spent the balance of his existence in endeavoring to straighten up his complicated affairs." Creditors, in the meantime, began dismantling the family's former empire. The beautiful mansions on Morrison were vacated. The lovely park was auctioned as a subdivision in 1857. The last vestige of the grandeur went in 1908: Page's mansion was razed and replaced by a row of flats.

(*Opposite Above*) Daniel D. Page mansion.
(*Opposite Below*) Parlor in Page mansion.

(*Above*) Henry D. Bacon mansion. One of the largest Greek Revival residences ever built in St. Louis. Note the hitching post in the lower left side of the picture.

Missouri Republican, June 8, 1857.

Page moved to a much simpler residence on the southeast corner of Sixth and Myrtle (now Clark) and lived there until 1865. His wife, Deborah, died January 19, 1864, of apoplexy and paralysis. She was in her seventy-fourth year. Page later married Jane Catherine Waters. They had a marriage contract specifying that each would keep his own property.

Page continued to work diligently to clear up the debts resulting from the collapse of his financial empire. He succeeded. At his death, April 29, 1869, his estate amounted to just $25,080.04--a sad remnant of a fortune which had earlier amounted to $1,500,000. Page and his first wife are buried in a most peculiar tomb in Bellefontaine Cemetery. His epitaph should read, "To build up and beautify the city of his adoption was his greatest ambition."

Bacon, not one easily daunted, returned to New York City in 1855 and arranged financing to complete his favorite project, the building of the Mississippi & Ohio Railroad. Back in St. Louis at his suite in Barnum's Hotel, he presided over the completion of the project that had ruined him

financially. In later years he moved to San Francisco, rebuilt his fortune, and became a leader in that community. Bacon died at Oakland, California, February 19, 1893. He was brought to St. Louis and interred in the Page tomb at Bellefontaine.

St. Louis had truly loved Page and Bacon. They had done much to build up the city. Their collapse had resulted from their trying to do too much too soon. The people admired them even more in their period of adversity, and rightfully so. Few men ever stood in higher regard among their contemporaries than had Page and Bacon.

James Harrison

James Harrison drove into St. Louis in 1840, heading straight for a bank. At the counter he explained what he required. The clerks looked at one another in amazement. One ran for an official. The officer, looking at the tall poker-faced individual of courtly bearing, thought Harrison hardly the type to be playing a joke. Walking up to him, he said, "I understand that you have a wagon full of money that you want to deposit?" Harrison replied, "Yes, all in coin. It will take several men to unload and move into your vault." After concluding his business, Harrison left the bank, already a celebrity in St. Louis. Though his entry to the city seemed somewhat dramatic to most, it was the Harrison style.

Born near Paris, Kentucky, October 10, 1803, Harrison spent his youth on a farm. He received a common school education, but under the best of circumstances he would never become a scholar. Harrison was practical in the extreme, and a man of action.

34

MISSOURI BANK NOTE & ENG CO. ST. LOUIS

Jas Hansen

35

When he was nineteen, James moved to Fayette, Missouri, and went into partnership with James Glasgow. They opened a store, but it was not to be an ordinary country store. Harrison, the adventurous one of the two, saw that fortunes were to be made in the West. He left to represent the firm in Sante Fe, New Mexico, living there for a number of years, channeling goods and trade back to Missouri. Glasgow remained at Fayette, and the partnership flourished.

In 1831 Harrison went south into Mexico and spent two years trading, principally in silver purchased from the mines of Jesus Maria. He transported the metal to Chihauhau and Mexico City through country infested with outlaws and hostile Indians. Attacks were frequent. On one expedition only Harrison and a friend escaped, the other eleven men being killed and scalped by Indians. The money was good, but the risks were high.

Having made a fortune in the Southwest, Harrison returned to Missouri. He was then engaged by the United States to help relocate the Indian tribes of Mississippi, Alabama, and Georgia. He was to move the tribes west of the Mississippi to country remote from the whites. This he did with deadly efficiency. Government contracts were then given to him to furnish these Indians with supplies. He moved to Fort Gibson, in Arkansas, and stayed three years. His contracts concluded in 1839. In the meantime, Harrison had become a very wealthy man. He then decided to move to St. Louis.

In 1840 Harrison and Glasgow opened the grocery firm of Gay, Glasgow & Company on Front Street near Vine (now St. Charles Street). Business was good, but Harrison dreamed of greater things. In 1843 he joined in partnership with Charles P. Chouteau and F. Vallé to purchase the Iron Mountain, a tremendous deposit of iron ore. By 1845 the American Iron Mountain Company had been formed, consisting of the above partners and others in Ste. Genevieve, Fredericktown, and New York City. They built furnaces and a rolling mill. Harrison was elected president of the company, and held that position until his death. The income from the business was incredible. Harrison's wealth increased to levels hitherto unknown in St. Louis. It was said, "Iron seemed to turn into gold at his touch."

Harrison later invested heavily in both the Iron Mountain Railroad and the Pacific Railroad, and was a director of both lines. Many other businesses drew his attention, and he was successful in all. By the 1860's he was worth over $3,000,000, and was the wealthiest citizen of St. Louis.

Harrison was a devoted family man. In December, 1830, he had married Maria Louisa Prewitt, of Howard County, Missouri. Like Harrison, she was a native of Kentucky. Mrs. Harrison accompanied her husband during his stay in Arkansas, but an army post could hardly be called a home. She was thus very happy when they moved to St. Louis and took up residence at 47 South Fourth Street.

In 1847 Harrison had built for her the most beautiful residence in St. Louis. People drove from miles around to see the grand house rise at the southwest corner of Eighth and Gratiot. Everything installed was the finest. The magnificent Corinthian portico was the crowning embellishment. When finished, the house stood as a gem of the Greek Revival.

Mrs. Harrison was not to enjoy her house for long. She died February 4, 1849, of pneumonia, leaving four young children. Her mother, Mrs. Mary McMillan Tremble Prewitt, then arrived and took charge of the household. Having heard the tales of her son-in-law's dangerous exploits in the Southwest, Mrs. Prewitt had a healthy respect for

The James Harrison mansion.

Indians. One day, as she sat in her room on the second floor, she heard the word, "How!" and thought that her end had come. There, standing before her, was an Indian. But, there was no danger. Amazed by the big house, the startled man had wandered in from the street, and had walked undetected into her room. He was quickly shown out.

The Harrison house had a beautiful view of the Mississippi River. The children of the household often amused themselves sitting on the grand porch, reading the names of passing steamboats. On the night of May 17, 1849, the view was particularly spectacular. The riverfront of St. Louis burned that night, and steamboats in flames could be seen drifting down the river, their names visible in the ghastly light. That night the northeast looked like the furnaces of Vulcan. A few years later houses were constructed across the street, forever blocking the river view.

The children often perched near the north windows, hoping to catch a glance of the famous Dr. McDowell, who lived and worked just across the street. Often they bragged to their playmates of the strange sights they had witnessed. Occasionally the Doctor caught sight of the movement of the lace curtains and directed a look their way, a look artfully mastered to frighten and belittle. A shriek would be heard as the children ran away, quickly followed by the Doctor's chuckle. Yes, it was a charming household for children, and young Edwin, the oldest of the Harrison children, and the only son, would sorely miss it when he was sent away to be educated in Belgium.

During the 1850's the block south of the Harrison house came to be the most fashionable in St. Louis. Fine mansions stretched south to Chouteau and around the corner. Behind, on Gratiot, the row was

37

almost equally as impressive. The names of the inhabitants read like a social register of St. Louis--Chouteau, Levering, Churchill, Knapp, Lackland, Brant, Vallé, Sol Smith, Treat, Priest, Paul, and on and on. Life was carefree. These were the rich, and St. Louis was theirs to enjoy.

When the Civil War came, this neighborhood fell into the midst of it. McDowell's hospital and college became a military prison. Houses were converted into army barracks, and troops constantly marched in the streets. The Harrison ladies often visited the military prison, taking small gifts to the inmates. Miss Dora Harrison struck up an acquaintance with a prisoner from South Carolina, Dr. Isaac Steedman. He was later to return to St. Louis, renew this friendship, and marry Dora Harrison.

James Harrison viewed the war with a sense of horror--it was a tragedy bordering on calamity. His friends and family were divided between North and South. The country he loved was being torn apart. At night, in the seclusion of his bedroom, Harrison often wept. One night he decided he had to take action himself. He would try to end the war.

Harrison went to Washington, D. C., and was received by President Lincoln. He stated that he had many friends among the officers of the Confederate Army, and he thought they could be persuaded to end the war if the proper terms were offered. Lincoln was impressed and issued him a pass to go into the South to conduct secret talks. Harrison did so. After meeting with officers in Arkansas, he returned to St. Louis. Hastily, he left for the Capitol.

Harrison arrived at the White House just as Lincoln was going out. The President told him he was engaged for the evening, but that he was very anxious to learn the results of his mission. He asked that Harrison take breakfast with him the next morning. As the President entered his carriage, he remarked that he was on his way to the theater to see *Our American Cousin*.

Harrison died, after a short illness, on August 2, 1870, and is buried at Bellefontaine Cemetery. Part of his obituary reads:

> Mr. Harrison possessed an indomitable energy, and with his native ability, clear judgment, and powerful will, he carried whatever he undertook to a successful termination. We have only cursorily glanced at the life of this estimable citizen. In looking back upon it, few can fail to realize that it is one of which any man can be proud. It is dignified by the successes which reward energy, and self reliance, and by the public benefits which it accomplished. Whilst the personal character of the man is unsullied through a long and active career, and was even completely free of a single vicious habit. It is such men that build up a city, and their deaths are public as well as private afflictions.

These great families of early St. Louis reflect the glory and the tragedy of those who dare to accept the challenge of their surroundings and take charge. They were alike in their efforts to build a greater and a more beautiful city. They were rarely conservative when the times and situations demanded action. They were men of vision who helped to create a city known for its wealth, beauty, and gracious way of life. They were empire builders, one and all.

Cafe au Lait Society

Stepping off his steamboat at St. Louis a visitor remarked, "Why, it looks like the third act of *The Octoroon*." Stretched before him was a scene of hundreds of Negroes driving mules which were pulling heavy cargoes up the steep incline from the wharf to the city above. Negro carriage drivers shouted, "Planter's House, Planter's House." Sable hucksters everywhere worked the milling crowds. It was truly a novel sight for the northern traveller first seeing this gateway to the South.

Proceeding up the narrow streets of the old French village to the American city above, the visitor had to marvel at the likes of "Old Rats," wandering the streets peddling his poisons from a greasy bag slung over his shoulder. Thundering through the streets came the voice of the town crier, Peter Hudson, shouting the names of lost children, for which service he charged five dollars in advance. A must for the curious sight-seer were the crowded Negro neighborhoods along Morgan Street (now Delmar). Beckoning to the less-timid with other needs to satisfy was the nearby and notorious Clabber Alley, a hellhole teeming with gamblers, prostitutes, and other assorted purveyors of vice. Thus, the St. Louis Negro quickly impressed the spectator both by his visibility and by his versatility.

However, there was a Negro society, well-known to the older inhabitants of the city, which was rarely revealed to the casual observer. This was a small class of Negro aristocrats whose ancestors had come to St. Louis with the French pioneers and had helped to create the city. They were French-speaking and were Catholic in religion. The

French liberality in racial matters had allowed them to flourish financially. They were respected and exercised considerable influence in older aristocratic circles. The leader of this group was Madame Pelagie Rutgers.

Madame Rutgers, attractive, rich, and bearer of one of the proudest names of St. Louis, was everything that a person of society in a Southern city should be, or almost so, for she was, in the polite terminology of that day, "a person of color." Little is known of her early years. She was born in St. Louis about 1804. Her mother, a slave, christened the child Pelagie Aillotte, but called her Eliza. Her probable father and owner, Jean Baptiste Aillotte, was a fur trader. He and his partner, François Beaupre, were killed on an expedition up the Missouri River in1808. Sometime later, this intelligent girl was able to purchase her freedom for the sum of three dollars, and marry St. Eutrope Clamorgan.

The Clamorgans were the one prominent family of creole days in St. Louis who could trace their ancestry to the tribes of Africa. The father of the clan was Jacques Clamorgan, businessman and

40

promoter extraordinaire. Of disputable origin, some say Welsh, he arrived in Upper Louisiana about 1784. He developed, even monopolized, the western trade of St. Louis and always commanded the ear of the Spanish Governors of Louisiana. Clamorgan never married, but in advanced years shocked the frontier town, fathering four children by three Negro women. In 1809, to guarantee their freedom, Jacques sold his children to their various mothers.

One of these children was St. Eutrope, born April 30, 1799, to Heleine. In 1820 St. Eutrope was one of the four barbers of St. Louis and had a shop on Main Street. On April 20 of that year, he married Pelagie Aillotte, and on June 21, she gave birth to Louise. That fall this young family went to St. Charles to take advantage of the trade generated by the session of the state legislature and remained there through February. Louise died during this stay in St. Charles. St. Eutrope died the following fall. Following the death of her family, Pelagie disappeared and did not come forward to claim her husband's estate until the summer of 1825. By the end of that year, her period of mourning was over.

Pelagie set her cap for the prize catch among the Negro bachelors of St. Louis, Louis Rutgers. Louis was the illegitimate mulatto son of the wealthy Dutch landowner, Arend Rutgers. Arend Rutgers, "a man scrupulously correct in all his intercourse with the world," recognized his child before all St. Louis. Louis was reared in the Rutgers household, and on January 31, 1826, received from his father "thirty arpents French measure" just south of St. Louis. Two days later Louis Rutgers and Pelagie Clamorgan were married.

The newly-married couple established their residence on this suburban property. Their house looked down an elevation to Carondelet Road (later known as Broadway) and was immediately north of City Cemetery, 5¼ acres at the northwest corner of Carondelet and Park, owned by Arend Rutgers. Louis served as sexton of the cemetery through the 1830's. After his father's death in 1837, Louis had trouble paying his debts and in 1840 was imprisoned.

Pelagie turned to her "next best friend," Louis Clamorgan, the nephew of her first husband, to protect the estate from creditors. Louis and Pelagie Rutgers deeded their lands temporarily to Clamorgan, who managed the property and restored order. In February, 1847, the inept Louis Rutgers died and was buried in Rock Springs Cemetery, a Catholic burial ground laid out amidst several beautiful groves of timber at the present southwest corner of Sarah and Duncan. Louis' white relatives stood beside Pelagie at the edge of the grave. They included his two half-sisters, Mrs. Marie Jeronima Provenchère and Sarah J. Rutgers. Also in attendance was his niece, Mrs. Mary Amelia Provenchère Maguire, wife of George Maguire, a former Mayor of St. Louis.

During the 1840's St. Louis expanded southward, greatly increasing the value of Pelagie's property. Seventh Street and Carondelet, the former piercing and the latter bordering her property, became major business arteries. City Cemetery, then poorly located, was closed and its bodies removed to Calvary and Bellefontaine. The Rutgers estate was ripe for development. Although Pelagie was illiterate, she had a fine head for business. She held on to her property and became a major landlord of St. Louis. Commercial buildings and tenements were erected on almost all her land; these she rented to white businessmen. Streetcars ran on Seventh Street, crowds thronged the sidewalks, and hucksters abounded. The noise of the neighborhood was great, but the money rolled in. Pelagie's income was enormous. Estimates of her wealth ran as high as $500,000, making her the

An 1863 view of the Rutgers estate. The mansion faced west and had a columned porch two stories high.

richest Negro in St. Louis, and advancing her into the first rank of wealth in the city. She now commanded the title of Madame Rutgers.

The Rutgers mansion and its grounds stood like an island in this teeming business community. The house, facing Seventh Street, was located on the north half of the block bordered by that street, Rutgers, Carondelet, and Park. Ancient trees shaded the dwelling, and a picturesque creek flowed along its north side. The interior was tastefully done in mahogany pieces, and dominated by a fabulous rosewood piano valued at one-third of the total furnishings. Another household fixture was Professor Gabriel Helms.

Professor Helms' relationship with Pelagie stretched back many years. Born in South Carolina in 1801, he moved to St. Louis in the spring of 1821 and began work as a barber. He met St. Eutrope and Pelagie during their sojourn in St. Charles. Helms and Pelagie remained close friends through the years. In the late 1850's he resided in her mansion and remained on the block until 1879. Gabriel Helms gained his nickname in the following manner:

> Some years ago, there came to our city a pompous little English dancing master, who hired Concert Hall and stuck up his name as "Professor Wells," teacher of the art and science of hop, skip and jump, particularly the waltz, or the science of genteel hugging.

Broadway looking north from Rutgers in 1872. French Market is in the center of the street in the background.

Helms had a shaving shop opposite the Hall, and he put up a sign with the name of "Professor Helms," in gold letters. The joke took, and Helms no doubt made many a dollar by the "take off."

Helms' daughter and her husband, Mr. Sawyer, boarded at the fashionable residence of P. G. Wells, a Negro minister, on Elm Street. Mrs. Sawyer was one of the most beautiful women of St. Louis. Well-educated and graced with considerable wit, "she...[was] the bright star of all social parties." Her visits to Madame Rutgers' household must have been eagerly awaited.

Antoinette, Pelagie's only child by Louis Rutgers, was born November 21, 1838. This was a very fortunate birth. For the first twelve years the Rutgers' union was childless. Had there been no issue, their property would have reverted to the legitimate heirs of Arend Rutgers. Antoinette received little formal education and never learned to play the rare piano in her mother's parlor. However, she was an attraction sufficient to catch the most eligible Negro bachelor in St. Louis, the handsome and genteel James P. Thomas.

Thomas, a man of the world, had known President James K. Polk and had been an intimate of that "gray-eyed man of destiny," William

Walker. He accompanied Walker in his conquest of Nicaragua, and after the British overthrow of that scheme, came to St. Louis and became a barber in the shop of the Clamorgans. It was probably this association which led to his introduction to Madame and Antoinette Rutgers.

In the nineteenth century it was not socially acceptable for a white man to serve as a barber in Southern communities. The better classes of whites always sought out Negro barbers. Thus, the most lucrative profession available to Negroes in that age was the tonsorial art. Thomas barbered on the steamboat William M. Morrison and later managed the shop at the palatial Lindell Hotel. He was thus employed when Pelagie Rutgers fell ill.

Sensing that her death was near, Pelagie centered her worries on the future of her daughter. It was imperative that Antoinette's fortune would be protected, and that could only be accomplished by the proper marriage. James P. Thomas was the answer. Although Antoinette had favored another, Pelagie saw that Thomas gained the inside track. Certain that their marriage would take place, Pelagie was at peace when she died February 22, 1867.

The little girl Eliza had gone a long way in life. It was Madame Rutgers that the six-horse hearse conveyed to Calvary Cemetery. Louis was moved to her plot from Rock Springs. Their tombstones have crumbled with age, but the lovely old bell tower still casts its shadow over their graves.

Antoinette married Thomas February 12, 1868,

Interior of St. Vincent de Paul Church at Ninth and Park.

at St. Vincent de Paul. The bride was lavishly arrayed. Her veil cost $900. The material in her dress cost $1,400. Her diamond earrings were valued at $5,000. All was splendor. To assure everyone that money was not his object for marriage, Thomas presented his bride with a check for $10,000. Newspapers reported his worth as up to $250,000. The great wealth of the young couple made them the subject of much gossip in the town, but the Thomases avoided much of it by going to Europe for an extended visit. There they saw all the sights familiar to Thomas from earlier trips.

In the late 1870's they moved to Alton, Illinois. Thomas continued in business in St. Louis as late as 1890, and Antoinette still held valuable properties in the city. She died in 1897. Her funeral was conducted from her mother's church, St. Vincent de Paul. She was buried beside her parents. James P. Thomas died in 1913 at age eighty-seven and was also interred at Calvary. Their descendants still reside in St. Louis.

The Clamorgans

Until her death Pelagie Rutgers maintained a close relationship with the Clamorgan family. Henry Clamorgan, another of St. Eutrope's nephews, settled near her in Frenchtown and helped to manage the Rutgers' estate after the death of Louis Clamorgan. The Clamorgans are worthy of further attention.

As previously noted, Jacques Clamorgan fathered four mulatto children--St. Eutrope, Appoline, Cyprian Martial, and Maximin. Jacques died November 11, 1814, at the age of eighty. His children, all minors, had first as a guardian John P. Cabanne and later Antoine P. Soulard. Of these children only Appoline was to continue the line.

Appoline Clamorgan, known as Pauline, was born February 7, 1803, to Suzanne (commonly known as Anne), a Negress. True to her father's example, she never married, but gave birth to seven children-- Cyprian Leon, Henry, Louis, Charles, Louisa, Pelagie Julie, and Cyprian. Her long-time lover, a prominent white man named Elias T. Langham, was probably the father of her children. He had been the administrator of the estate of St. Eutrope, her brother. Pauline Clamorgan died May 1, 1830, of complications in childbirth. She was buried in white silk. Her estate, consisting of a stone residence and rental properties in what is now called Laclede's Landing, also included a small volume entitled "Pauline Clamorgan's Memorandum Book." Her surviving children were Henry, Louis, Louisa, and Cyprian. Clamorgan Alley in that neighborhood now serves as a reminder of the family.

Henry, born in 1823 and the eldest of the surviving Clamorgan children, began his career as a boatman on the Mississippi, but by 1848 he had become a barber. As his brother Cyprian wrote:

> A mulatto takes to razors and soap as naturally as a young duck to a pool of water, or a strapped Frenchman to dancing; they certainly make the best barbers in the world, and were doubtless intended by nature for the art. In its exercise, they take white men by the nose without giving offense, and without causing an effusion of blood.

By 1852 his shop was located at the northwest corner of Fourth and Pine; he would continue in business there until his death on March 9, 1883. His partners at various times included Byertere Hickman, Samuel Mordecai, and his brothers, Louis and Cyprian.

The tonsorial palace of H. Clamorgan & Co. was superior to any other in St. Louis and the equal of any in the nation. It consisted of ten large, airy, and elegantly furnished bathrooms, each equipped with a tub of the finest Italian marble and a large mirror. The water was "as clear as crystal." There were six mahogany barber chairs, and light was supplied from three bronze chandeliers. The customary iron barber pole stood outside. Adjacent to the bath and barbershop was the beautiful perfumery and fancy goods store, usually presided over by Louis Clamorgan, of whom it was said, "He understands how to gratify the fancy tastes of ladies and gentlemen better than any man we know." The stock of perfumes, ladies' and gentlemen's dressing cases, and toilet ware was the finest selection in St. Louis. Unfortunately, a fire destroyed this shop September 5, 1853. However, the business of the baths and barbershop was not interrupted. Those who visited the Clamorgans left feeling pampered and pleased and considerably poorer. Elegance did have its price.

Henry Clamorgan married Harriet Eagleson in 1842. Theirs was a relatively happy life until the fall of 1851. Tragedy then struck in the most appalling manner. One of their children died each month from October through January. Harriet grieved for the children until her death in 1855. A single marker in Calvary Cemetery serves as their monument. Inscribed are the words:

> Erected by an affection-
> ate husband and father,
> may they rest in peace.

Henry remarried in 1859, this time to a mulatto named Amanda Woodside. They settled on the east side of Eighth Street south of Hickory. In later years the family moved to the southwest corner of Chippewa and Iowa where they lived the remainder of the century.

Louis Clamorgan, Pelagie Rutgers' "next best friend," married Julia M. Knight on September 17, 1840. In 1844 he was a barber in the partnership of Clamorgan and Moses. The following year he operated the Italian Baths as part of the partnership of Iredell and Clamorgan. He then merged his business with that of his brother, Henry. Louis died in December, 1851. His widow and children, Leon and Julius, were watched over by Madame Rutgers. They were moved to a house just around the corner from Pelagie's mansion.

The most fascinating of the Clamorgans was Appoline's last child, Cyprian, born April 24, 1830. Like his brothers he became a barber and followed that profession from 1848 through the early 1850's. His gossipy nature made him a natural for such a business. Later he put the tales he often spoke on paper and in 1858 published that remarkable small book, *The Colored Aristocracy of St. Louis*. Filled with catty descriptions of prominent Negroes, recountings of tales most had hoped were long forgotten, and frequent references about the morals of various individuals, the book caused an uproar which Cyprian should have anticipated. Of Madame Rutgers he remarked:

> [She is] a brown-skinned straight-haired woman of about fifty years of age; she is large, fine-looking, and healthy, and has been quite handsome....Mrs. R. is a member of the Catholic church, but is not noted for her piety; she worships the almighty dollar more than Almighty God. She makes a fine appearance in society, but, exposes her ignorance when she attempts to converse.

The book is a remarkable work, but its reception, along with his arrest in May, 1860, on a charge of forgery, probably encouraged him to take his wife, the former Joanne E. Stewart, and move to New

Orleans. They departed St. Louis at the beginning of the Civil War and only occasionally returned from the Crescent City. There he became a leader in the Negro community.

An excellent example of the wit and style of Cyprian Clamorgan is a sketch he wrote about another Negro of Frenchtown, Samuel Mordecai, the next door neighbor of Henry Clamorgan.

> Although his name indicates a Jewish origin, we are not aware that Sam has any aversion to pork, or would hesitate to sit down to a game of "poker" on Saturday. He is one of the wealthiest of our colored aristocracy, and is good for one hundred thousand dollars when "Flush." He is an ardent votary of the blind goddess, and has been one of her prime favorites; he made the greater portion of his fortune by the turn of cards, and is the most inveterate gambler we have ever met with. He has an incurable passion for games of chance, and will bet his pile on anything that has the appearance of uncertainty. From the simple trick of the thimble rigger or Mexican puzzle to a horse race or Presidential election, Mordecai is always "in." He lives at his ease, but is interested in business at the corner of Fourth and Pine streets. For many years he was a steward on the river, and is one of the most energetic business men to be met with anywhere. Mordecai is a Kentuckian by birth, and has inherited many of the good qualities of the sons of that noble State; he is extremely polite in his intercourse with his equals and inferiors, and quite aristocratic in his feelings. He came here about sixteen years ago, and has prospered ever since. He has an interesting daughter, fifteen years of age, who is at school in England. He is a man of general information, and has travelled a great deal; he talks seriously of taking up his abode in Paris, on the completion of his daughter's education.

The Clamorgan brothers thought they had inherited little other than an illustrious family tradition. However, in the 1850's a long-forgotten asset was rediscovered. In 1805, their grandfather, Jacques Clamorgan, had acquired Regis Loisel's right to 38,111 acres of United States territory. In 1813 Clamorgan conveyed the same to his two sons, Cyprian and Maximin. These sons left no heirs other than the children of their sister, Appoline. Thus, on June 2, 1858, the United States' Congress confirmed the above property to the Clamorgan heirs. In 1863 they settled for 38,111 acres in the Kansas Territory. This windfall made the Clamorgans the talk of the town and stirred many memories of their grandfather, the empire-builder, Jacques.

The Clamorgans, even more than their Rutgers allies, were readily accepted by the white business community. They were aided in this respect by the fact that they were virtually white themselves. Cyprian Clamorgan might well have been speaking of his family when he wrote, "Many of them were separated from the white race by a line of division so faint that it could be traced only by the keen eye of prejudice." Indeed, that trace was so faint that in the early twentieth century the Clamorgans moved away from St. Louis and have since passed undetected as whites.

Sarah Hazlett

The Rutgers and Clamorgans were famous in the business world of St. Louis and were well-known to the public. However, one of the most intriguing Negroes of nineteenth-century St. Louis shunned publicity and was the rich, beautiful, and elusive

Mrs. Sarah Hazlett. Who her forebears were is not known, but they were from the first rank of St. Louis' white society, and they provided for her amply. Everyone, white and black, acknowledged her as an aristocrat. She swept through the streets with an imperious air and associated with few. Fewer still, outside of those admitted to whispered gossip in the grand old homes of the French pioneers, knew the secrets of her background--secrets they all took to the grave. Who was she? What was the source of her wealth? Why was she treated as something quite apart and special by the French aristocracy? Probably no one will ever know, for she was an enigma in her own time.

She was married to Monroe Hazlett, a boatman. They lived on the south side of Clark Street, between Eighth and Ninth. Two daughters were born to the union, Theodosia and Emily. Both girls inherited their mother's beauty and wit and were sent to Philadelphia to be educated. That city was then renowned for its educational facilities for free Negroes. Just when Sarah and Monroe Hazlett parted is not known. In 1854 he was in St. Louis to claim the estate of his mother, Mary Hazlett. It was a modest sum, but it included the house on Clark Street, comfortably furnished and equipped with a small library.

In 1858 Cyprian Clamorgan described Sarah as,

> a fascinating "grass widow," upon whose features time has left the trace of beauty, though fast falling into the "sere and yellow;" she is about thirty-five years of age and possesses a comfortable fortune of seventy thousand dollars. A mystery hangs over the gay widow, which curious eyes have in vain endeavored to penetrate.

Sarah and her daughters lived on Franklin Avenue, between Sixth and Seventh in "grand style." Just how grand was the Hazlett's lifestyle came to be appreciated by all of St. Louis in the summer of 1860. That was when the wedding of the century took place.

Theodosia developed into an incredible beauty and bore no trace of Negro blood. Cyprian Clamorgan said that she was a "marigold of beauty." He further stated:

> She has it in her power to choose a husband from amongst the best of her class, and but for the prejudice of caste in this country, many a white man would be found sighing at her feet; her form is the perfection of youthful grace, and her dark lustrous eyes would shame the orbs of the wild gazelle.

Just whom she chose was Felix Dora, the son of Mrs. Nancy Lyons. Mrs. Lyons, once a milliner, later the owner of an "aristocratic" boarding house on Sixth Street near Gratiot, lived then on the northeast corner of Orchard and Eleventh. She was the widow of Charles Lyons, who had perished in the California gold rush. She was a most successful businesswoman and had acquired a modest fortune.

Sarah had to have the best for her daughter, and that was what she got. The site chosen for the wedding was the Catholic Cathedral. Father Ryan would officiate. Invitations were hand-delivered to the residences of the old French families, and all were accepted. On June 12, 1860, the huge array of carriages converged on the magnificent church, and it was soon packed with nearly one thousand persons, "known as among the oldest white families in the city."

The twenty-four-year-old groom cut a dashing figure, but all eyes were on the exquisite bride. Seventeen-year-old Theodosia was dressed to perfection. The St. Louis *Evening News* reported:

> The Bride wore a very rich brocade silk, double flounced,

pure silvery white, elegantly woven, of a single pattern. It set her regal form splendid. Her hair was dressed a la Imperatrice, crowned with a wreath of orange flowers that was woven with such artistic skill it looked tribute of a thousand bowers. The veil was tulle, of gossamer fineness. Jewels rich and rare [the *Missouri Republican* described them as "a dazzling profusion of diamonds"] sparkled here and there...The jewels were family heirlooms.... Her family are old and distinguished citizens of historical fame.

The Catholic Cathedral

After the wedding 250 invited guests went from the Cathedral to a fantastic party at the home of the mother of the groom. "Wit, mirth and the mazy dance consumed the night." The next day the groom entertained hundreds of friends. "The callers were coming and going all day. It was hospitality on the grandest scale."

The *Missouri Republican* reported that the "colored population" of the city would in future use the "stupendous" wedding as an "epoc to date from." That paper used the terms "darkey" and "sables" in describing members of the wedding party. In reply Sarah Hazlett and Nancy Lyons wrote:

Sir, whilst we are the recipient of your lengthy and much exaggerated notice, we feel that it would be humiliating and, in fact, criminal in us to let it go to the public without our earnest protest. Sir, the persons referred to are neither "darkies" nor "sables," and we feel proud that our wedding was honored with the presence of a thousand persons, the majority of whom were some of the first families of this city.

This fact, to which we appeal, will bear us out in the assertion that had your reporter not heard that we belonged to the colored race, he never would have known it from our appearance.

The offended *Missouri Republican* later replied, "We have in St. Louis the sassiest and most arrogant set of free niggers in America probably." To that remark the two mothers remained mute.

Felix and Theodosia Dora moved to 39 Paul Street, that beautiful avenue just south of Chouteau. Their neighbors were the elite of society. For a time Felix was a steward, but he soon opened his own restaurant. At one time he was located in the depot of the S.L.K.C. & N. Railroad. In the 1880's he gave up the restaurant business and went into partnership with the famous James P. Thomas. They operated a barbershop at 615 Washington Avenue. It is hoped that life for this beautiful couple was as happy as their beginning showed promise.

Several other Negro barbers and businessmen lived in the neighborhood dominated by Madame Rutgers. As previously mentioned, this closely-knit group was allied with the old French and American society. This connection assured for these Negroes privileges almost unheard of elsewhere in the nation. They attended church with their white neighbors at St. Vincent de Paul. Before they had the franchise, they used their wealth to sway voters and politicians to serve their needs. Laws designed to restrict Negroes were not enforced against this privileged class. In the latter part of the nineteenth and in the early part of the twentieth centuries, their children, with special permission, attended classes in the white schools of St. Louis. In short, these Negro families constituted the elite of that aristocracy so charmingly described by Cyprian Clamorgan. When James P. Thomas and Antoinette moved to Alton, the Negro elite started to drift away from Frenchtown. By the turn of the century, this choice Negro neighborhood had vanished.

The Peculiar Institution

Few Negroes of St. Louis enjoyed the advantages of the Rutgers or Clamorgans. Slavery was the way of life for most, and that institution was firmly established in Frenchtown. However, it was the

The Negro nurses stroll on the sidewalks, chattering in quaint French to the little children.

kinder side of slavery that was most evident in the area. Few slaves were employed in the neighborhood in any capacity other than as house servants, and the mansions in which they served were generally inhabited by reasonable masters. There is a disputed story of Daniel D. Page beating two of his slaves. Most of the larger mansions were staffed by four slaves. An exception was the residence of John G. Priest and Virginia Chouteau, where sixteen slaves were required. Some slaves of the area were quite skilled. Nerée Vallé, another Chouteau son-in-law, surprised his wife by giving her a personal hairdresser. This slave, Marie, had been sent to New Orleans for a two-year apprenticeship under the famous Jerome Merlin.

The slave-owning aristocracy of Frenchtown usually inherited whatever staff was needed for their homes, but occasionally additional servants had to be purchased or rented. Homeowners usually went to B. M. Lynch who made a specialty of handling house servants. His stalls on Locust between Fourth and Fifth streets were always well stocked.

The Germans who moved into Frenchtown during the 1850's did not make use of Negro labor, slave or free. Their households and firms were run by newly arrived immigrants. The German press of St. Louis, led by Frenchtown residents, was unswerving in its opposition to the "peculiar institution."

The Negro aristocrats of Frenchtown also refrained from owning slaves. It must have been extremely painful for those proud people to see members of their own race owned by their very neighbors. However, these Negro businessmen did little to oppose the institution, probably realizing the futility of such action and the resulting damage such a stand would have inflicted on their various businesses.

Happy Hollow

Happy Hollow represented the other extreme of Negro society in Frenchtown. It was located on the northern edge of the area, in the block bordered by Gratiot, Sixth, Papin, and Seventh streets. There a sycamore-bordered ravine carried the water from Chouteau's Pond after it passed over the dam or wheel of the mill. The ravine dropped thirty feet below the surrounding area. In the earlier years it had been the resort of the Negro laundresses of the city. On Mondays the crowds of women and children filled the area, and laughter and good times were the order of the day. However, all things come to an end.

By the late 1840's the ravine had become filled with about a dozen shacks inhabited by battling free Negroes and poor whites, and police were on a first-name basis with most of the inhabitants. Happy Hollow was everything that the Rutgers neighborhood was not; filth and vice ruled the polluted ravine. Its odd name did not result from laundresses waxing nostalgic, as some writers have suggested. The truth is, this filthy region was one of the few areas of St. Louis spared during the great cholera epidemic of 1849; the astounded inhabitants and neighbors thus named the gulley "Happy Hollow." In the late 1860's the waters of Mill Creek were routed through an emormous sewer, the depression was filled, and business houses were erected on the site. Happy Hollow was no more.

*****

A cook shopping in the streets.

One hundred years have passed since the decline and disappearance of the Negro neighborhoods of Frenchtown. Time has erased even the memory of the inhabitants, be they noble or deplorable. What facts do survive are as scattered and fragmented as a shattered mosaic. But, the bits and pieces of the tale suffice to destroy the stereotype image of nineteenth-century St. Louis Negroes. Yes, the Negro community of that era was every bit as varied as that of the whites. They had their businessmen, writers, and friends of national leaders. They also had their thieves, bums, and cutthroats. And strange though it was, Frenchtown Negroes seem to have been in the vanguard of all these fields. They were the best and the worst of a fascinating lot.

Happy Hollow in foreground. Carriage is headed north on Seventh Street. McDowell's Medical School is in the rear.

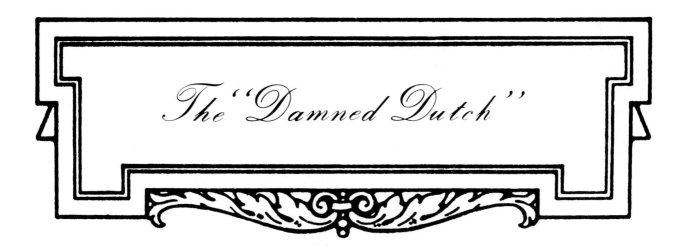

The "Damned Dutch"

My God! You have to speak German just to buy a ticket on the streetcar! Everywhere you turn, you see them: Germans--stumbling up street, down street, cross street! "Umpapa" bands, singing societies, and visiting on Sundays! And every day it gets worse! Take a walk to the wharf and at almost any hour, boats can be seen unloading their hoards of Germans! When will it ever end! Thus mused the bewildered French and Americans as they saw their beloved St. Louis of the 1850's being transformed into what they feared would become one giant, crowded beer hall!

Formerly, the French farmers and traders of early St. Louis had lived quietly and comfortably on their spacious lands overlooking the wide river. The land had held a few small towns, scattered villages and single farms limited in number, but settled like the entire great West--more or less a wilderness: seldom penetrated by a white man, and perhaps never by a German!

The first immigration of Germans between 1663 and the Revolutionary War of 1775 had populated vast regions of Virginia, Pennsylvania, Maryland, and New York, with settlements in the Carolinas and Georgia--but none further west. Henry S. Geyer, the soon-to-be-prominent St. Louisan born in 1790 of German parentage in Maryland, had reached this French community--but as an Anglo-American, not a German émigré. For that 12-year period of German immigration had ceased altogether in 1775, and would not resume until the end of the Napoleonic wars--a 50-year period long enough to break any connection between the earlier and later immigrations. Thus far, St. Louis had seen no direct settlement by Germans.

Meanwhile, a patriotic spirit among the German people had recruited the sizable armies needed in the campaigns against Napoleon in 1814 and 1815. The Germans had seen the hope of securing national unity and liberal domestic policies, and had given to the armies virtually every German male--from the teenaged youth to the gray-haired veteran. Yet, these victorious armies had brought severe disappointments to their people. At the end of the conflicts, the crowned heads of Austria, the German states, and Russia, meeting in the Congress of Vienna, had decided to maintain their kingly authority and to repress all manifestations of liberalism. Now re-instated, the thirty-six German potentates had curtailed freedom of speech and had maintained a rigid censorship of the press. The hope of greater freedom for the German people had been crushed by the re-imposition of ruling authority. Lost in their own victories, the German people faced mounting frustrations over the control of their own destiny.

The light flow of German immigrants between 1820 and 1830, however, did bring to Missouri the first representative of this frustrated people who sought his own paradise in the hinterlands of America. Dr. Gottfried Duden, who arrived in St. Louis in 1824, intended to become a farmer. This highly intelligent man with a classic education had held several prominent positions in the Prussian government, but had left his native land to find a better life "...under the western sky of the New World."

This educated man of little practical insight purchased land north of the Missouri River in Montgomery (now Warren) County and settled on a farm, where he wrote glowing descriptions about Missouri in letters to the Fatherland. Duden's writing so impressed those in Germany, where he was well-known and respected, that men, women, and children who had never thought of leaving their homeland resolved to emigrate to this paradise. Duden's accounts caused the formation of the Giessener Emigration Society, organized in 1833, to aid emigrants from Germany. At this time both the educated classes and the youth felt a deep dissatisfaction with their Napoleonic war efforts, coupled with several years of partial crop failures. Mutterings of discontent were loud and universal throughout western Europe. It was a year of unrest and uprisings. It was 1830.

This period of German immigration, the first to reach St. Louis, brought the educated man of Duden's stature: men of learning and standing in their communities--physicians, lawyers, clergymen, teachers, artists, merchants, officials--professional men of all branches:

54

They had wielded the pen, but never handled the hoe; they had stood in the pulpit, but never behind the plow; they had lectured from the cathedral and pleaded in court, but had never driven an ox team; they were but little prepared for the hardships that were in store for them, but they brought with them a sufficient energy and perseverance, diligence and frugality, to overcome most of the obstacles they had to encounter. They changed barren land into green meadows, stony acres into grain-growing fields and fruit-bearing orchards; they cultivated the soil and did much towards making Missouri an agricultural, horticultural, and even wine-producing State.

Duden's letters had set the stage, but the political problems facing Germans had been the prime moving force. The second tide of German settlement had started, following the dictates of Duden the Idealist.

It is ironic, however, that Dr. Gottfried Duden, hampered by personal illness during his almost three-year stay, moving between St. Louis and his farm in Montgomery County, was forced to return to Germany. There, in his homeland, he collected his letters into book form and circulated widely his own treatise extolling the virtues of a paradise he himself could not enjoy. Yet, in his mind's eye, this bountiful region offered a future to the German seeking to express his own free will in a free land.

St. Louis received its fair share from this period of immigration. In twenty years (1830-1850), the population of the city grew from 7,000 to 77,860. By 1850 the St. Louis census showed 36,529 native Americans and 38,397 foreign born; from the latter number, 22,340 had been born in Germany.

The educated leadership that found its way from the German hinterland to the American heartland brought to St. Louis a diversity in talent that would ennoble a growing community. This influx of new citizens was a selective one and prestigious. And others writing in the Duden vein would set a second stage for more German immigrants to come to the area. But this time, they would choose St. Louis first rather than try farming first, and this time, they would select a particular spot:

> According to the local (city) census of 1852, so much of the southern end of the city as was embraced in what was then the First Ward, contained 13,779 inhabitants, of whom 12,038 were Germans.

And this group would be known as the "Fortyeighters."

This period of German immigration, the second and by far the largest to reach St. Louis, stemmed from the revolutionary movements of 1848 and 1849 in France, Germany, and Austria, and included both the professional people of the previous wave along with the mechanics, peasants, journeymen, and laborers of all classes--all coming to make this country their home, and to become citizens of "...the greatest Republic on earth."

The growing numbers seemed incredible to the local citizens as these German immigrants swept over this relatively small city. Throughout the 1850's came daily arrivals of the Fortyeighters, so numerous by 1854 that the *Missouri Republican* of February 15 was forced to comment:

> Three or four of the last boats up have brought large numbers of German emigrants. The Kennett had on board 300 or more, the H. D. Bacon over 100, and the Elephant about the same number. They are generally a hard looking set, sickly looking, dirty and poorly clad. Take them "all in all," they resemble the breaking up of a hard winter. But it is thought that when the spring sun comes out and they get themselves cleaned up and their hair cut off, they will look quite as respectable as other people.

This German element in the new wave was in such great preponderance among the newcomers that at least part of the city became Germanized. The proverbial industry, patience, and frugality of the German mechanic and laborer spelled their success in a foreign country. These qualities had assured them of employment and had made them well-liked in earlier days, but now their great numbers swelled St. Louis with such different attitudes and mannerisms so quickly that established residents feared for the future of their city.

The one saving grace most accorded the Germans was their marvelous ability to manufacture beer. St. Louisans quickly became addicted to the brew, and the taverns became crowded with "boys rushing from the bar to the tables with more glasses of beer than it would seem within the power of two hands to carry." So complete was St. Louis' infatuation with this "barley water" that from March 1st to September 1st, 1854, over eighteen million glasses were consumed in the city--an amount requiring the expenditure of nearly a million dollars. Thirty breweries were necessary to supply the city and its surrounding area. They

Northwest corner of Eighth and Lafayette (then Soulard) in the 1890's. Typical of the German tenements in Frenchtown.

German children on South Broadway in the 1890's. Note the lunch pail on the boy's arm.

were:

Arsenal	New Bremen
Bellefontaine	Oregon
Eagle	Philadelphia
English & Gilpin	Pittsburgh
Excelsior	Rocky Branch
Franklin	Salvador
Fritz, Wainwright & Co.	Schnaiders'
Hammers'	Schneiders'
Iron Mountain	Schuerr's
Jackson	Steam Brewery
Lafayette	Stifels
Laurel	Stumpfs'
Lemp's	Uhrigs'
Mound	Wash Street
National	Winkelmeyers'

The large number of breweries persisted in St. Louis throughout the century. After Cherokee Cave was discovered at Cherokee and Carondelet Road, in February, 1866, many of the breweries located in that vicinity to take advantage of the cool cavern's storage space. However, the magic of beer could not erase the fact of German encroachment in all other ways of life, and that was where the problem lay.

Frenchtown almost groaned beneath its ponderous German weight. Gerry-built shacks lined its

1890's view of a German neighborhood just off South Broadway.

various alleys, crowding close to what were the elegant avenues of the day. People were crammed into every available space. Small tight attics did yeoman service housing minor clerks and laborers. Unfortunates were forced to seek shelter wherever they could. One tragic death notice was that of Franz Carl Pollot who suffocated in the hot confines of his garret at Seventh and Rutgers. The crowded living conditions--outdoor toilets, immediately adjacent to wells, with garbage everywhere present--sent the aroma of the Frenchtown Germans into the very houses of their French and American neighbors. To have had an acute sense of smell in that era was to suffer worse than those

having lost a limb.

Children were forced to use the streets and alleys as their playgrounds, often with tragic results. The new streetcars plowing their way through this mass of humanity took a heavy toll of limbs and lives. Frequent were such notices as the following:

An inquest was yesterday held in a tenement on Carondelet avenue, just south of Hickory street, in view of the dead body of Geo. Schulter, a child nearly 3 years of age....On the previous afternoon the child was with several other little ones at play in the street, floating little boats in the gutter opposite his parents' residence. In the vicinity, the horse of Mr. Blum, attached to a

Northeast corner of Seventh and Lafayette (then Soulard) in the 1890's. Lafayette and Soulard street names have since been exchanged.

light spring wagon, became uncontrollably fractious, and in rearing and plunging, threw one of his fore legs over the shaft. He was thus tripped, and fell with his breast against the child, crushing him to death against an awning post. The injuries were a rupture of the vital organs of the chest and abdomen. The jury of inquest rendered it as their verdict that the death was accidentally caused in the manner we have stated.

"Yellow journalism" in local papers played upon the fears of the establishment, emphasizing German crime, emotional instability, and political unrest. Such coverage featured frequent suicides, tavern brawls, and gruesome murders. Several Germans were reported to have jumped into open wells. Often, women reported being accosted at the French Market, Frenchtown's popular shopping area in the middle of Broadway at Chouteau avenue; the area supposedly abounded with thieves, cutthroats, and abandoned children (known as "Street Arabs"), and most of them speaking with a German accent:

An Incorrigible Youngster--The most positive specimen of the class Young America came to the lower police station yesterday about noon. He is apparently not over five years old--not old enough to make his speech intelligible--and when we saw him he was smoking a chalk pipe

Paulus Röetter's drawing of Sixth and Hickory, looking west. The small building with a cupola was a German school later used by Negroes.

with a stem about an inch long, the fumes of which were strong enough to poison an anaconda. He swears, chews tobacco, drinks beer and whisky, has been several times drunk, and was very importunate for a "drink" while at the station house; he waltzes and "jigs," and gave a specimen of his terpsichorean accomplishment. As near as he could be understood, his name is Johnny Ather, and he lives in the neighborhood of the French Market. We pronounce him absolutely a lost boy. He is now at the Central police station on Chestnut street, and seems sufficiently a "man of the world" to be at home anywhere.

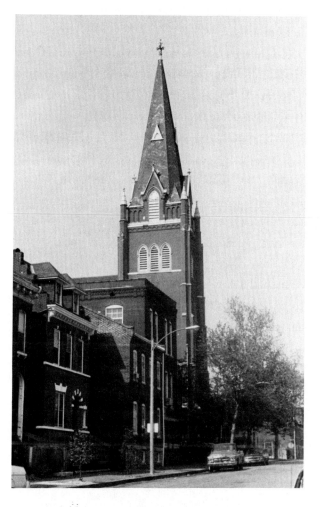

Trinity Lutheran Church. Eighth and Soulard. Mother church of Missouri Synod.

Domestic squabbles between Germans found their way into daily reporting; so did the emotional upsets with their bizarre details:

A German woman named Elizabeth Kramer, who has been for some time addicted to drinking, and who lived on Chouteau Avenue, between Sixth and Seventh streets, fell down stairs last Friday evening, and though only slightly injured, died at 11 o'clock the same night. Her injuries were not sufficient to account for her death, and the coroner's jury yesterday morning returned a verdict that she died from intemperance. Her husband, who is as worthless and intemperate as was his wife, declined to bury her, and although she died on Friday night she had not been interred yesterday morning [the Monday following] and the Coroner receiving a call to hold an inquest on her body was compelled to have her buried. Kramer, even when the Coroner was about to have her disposed of, objected, and alleged that he wanted to keep her. Since her death he has passed his time along side of the dead body, and neighbors state that they saw him taking numerous pitchers of lager beer into the cellar, where she lay, and where he steeped his senses in the combined odors of malt and putrification. Old Kramer kept drinking his beer and watching his wife until yesterday morning. When the Coroner arrived so far had the body advanced in decomposition that it was almost impossible for the jury to remain long enough in the room for the purpose of giving it the usual inspection.

The French and American aristocrats who lived only a block up the street surveyed this scene with disgust, and one passerby insisted he heard Mrs. Paul's muffled comment, "The Damned Dutch!"

These stories were read with morbid fascination, but more frightening were reports of street riots and election frauds, the most dramatic of which happened Monday, April 5, 1852, between the Germans and Americans. Germans took possession of the polls at Soulard Market to prevent the opposition from voting. Those who tried to break through the crowd were driven back with sticks and stones; even Mayor Luther Kennett, one of the candidates, was "roughly handled." When information reached four other wards, about 3:00 p.m., a group of native-born and adopted Americans numbering over 5,000 moved down to the polls at Soulard Market. The densely-packed Germans holding the area made repeated attacks on the crowd, "...throwing stones and other missiles into it, while an occasional shot was fired from the windows of the houses." However, a force of 200 well-armed Americans reached the market and, "...with a shout for 'free suffrage,' " charged the Germans and opened the polls again to all voters. Germans continued firing on the crowd from neighboring houses, which forced the crowd to riddle Soulard Market and Neumeyer's Tavern (located at 7th and Park). When a fireman was killed by a shot fired from the tavern, the enraged

Americans stormed Neumeyer's and burned it down. The rioting continued until dark, when the mob placed two six-pounders on the corner of Park Avenue, "...so as to sweep the sidewalks, where large crowds of Germans had gathered." However, the cannons were not fired; instead, the groups hurled stones and brickbats at each other until several influential persons intervened. About 10:00 p.m. another mob of about 1,500 people gathered in front of the *Anzeiger des Westens* printing office, in resentment over certain articles that had appeared in the paper; however, Mayor Kennett sent two companies of city military to surround the building, and later the crowd dispersed, following a day and night of grief.

St. Louisans truly looked with alarm at their new inhabitants. The southern sections of Frenchtown were rapidly becoming a bastion of German culture. By 1859 the population breakdown of the city shows 131,858 whites, composed of 59,714 Americans, 43,655 Germans, 22,011 Irish, 3,441 English, 1,215 French, and 4,986 others. And the Irish taking north sections of the city were being viewed as fearfully as were the Germans taking the south sections of St. Louis. Reflecting on such, many wondered what neighborhoods would be next. What had taken others decades to achieve in St. Louis had almost overnight passed into the hands of the Germans!

But responding to this local threat were the Know-Nothings and that colorful speaker, Joseph Nash McDowell, St. Louis' Self-Appointed Protector Against the Teutonic Peril!

Sts. Peter and Paul Church in 1888.

The Eccentric Genius

"Roll the cannon out! Prepare to fire! We'll show those papist bastards what it's like to tangle with Dr. Joseph Nash McDowell!"

"But Sir, there are hundreds of them, and they're armed!"

"Who gives a damn! What if there are a few hundred! Kill them all; the world will be better off! Don't argue! Roll the cannon out and prepare to fire!"

A typical day in the life of Dr. McDowell? Incredibly, Yes! There were few calm moments in the life of that eccentric genius. Controversy seemed to stalk him. He delighted, he frightened, he was loved, he was hated, but he was never ignored. A mention of his name evoked a mass of contradictory statements.

After Dr. McDowell came to St. Louis, nothing was ever the same again. For almost three decades he was the most notorious citizen of St. Louis. Everyone was quick to admit that he was a genius at the surgical table--but otherwise? "You know the man is quite mad!" "Did you hear what he said yesterday?" "Did you hear what he did the day before?" And so it went. McDowell was always the center of attention, and he enjoyed every minute of it. Henry Clay thought McDowell "had the greatest mind on earth except for its eccentricities." Surviving accounts are so incredible that it is almost impossible to discern the man enshrouded in the legend.

Dr. McDowell, already renowned in the field of medicine, arrived in St. Louis in March, 1840. He was the nephew of the famous Dr. Ephraim McDowell of Kentucky, and had made quite a name for himself teaching anatomy at the Cincinnati Medical College. His students said he could "make even the dry bones speak." Soon after arriving here, he took the lead in establishing a medical school. It was affiliated with Kemper College, an Episcopalian institution. On June 11, 1840, McDowell laid the cornerstone for a medical building near the southwest corner of Ninth and Cerre streets. The impressive Greek Revival structure, facing east, was finished that fall, and classes began the first week in November. The students were required to be twenty-one years of age and be of good moral character. The term would close the last of February.

The brick building housed a well-equipped school. An amphitheater seated five hundred. The gallery of the amphitheater housed the anatomical museum and library. The chemical laboratory and the

Kemper College Medical College. Chouteau's Pond in background.

common lecture room could each hold five hundred students. The two dissecting rooms, located in the attic, were forty-five feet long. An octagonal observatory, equipped with a telescope, surmounted the building. Near the college, on Ninth Street, was a surgical infirmary where patients were treated. The site was picturesque, located on the southern shore of Chouteau's Pond. But, even more important, it was remote from the city, and yet not too removed from several cemeteries.

Soon the rumors began. Bodies were being stolen from the cemeteries and carved up by the mad doctor. Some people scoffed, but others said that they had seen things in the night that would chill

men's souls. Some joked, "Don't go too near the college, or you might end up as a classroom assignment." Those whose journeys did take them near the site walked faster and crossed themselves, especially if it was night.

The rumors were only too true. McDowell's only dependable supply of bodies came from fresh burials. Often at night a group of students, accompanied by the doctor, would steal into City Cemetery or St. Vincent's with their shovels in hand. These "resurrectionists" struck terror into the hearts of those families mourning recent deaths. It was inevitable that clashes would result.

In 1845, due to difficulties in financing the

institution, Dr. McDowell's College was affiliated with the state university and renamed the Missouri Medical College. However, most still referred to it as McDowell's College. The enrollment of 160 in 1846 was the greatest ever. After the cholera epidemic of 1849, enrollments throughout the fifties averaged slightly over one hundred. These students were drawn from the surrounding states and the South. McDowell's College was the second largest medical school in the Mississippi Valley.

Near the end of October, 1849, a new building, under construction since 1847, was rushed to completion. It was the largest structure devoted to medical science in the United States, and was a most peculiar work of architecture. It rose at the northwest corner of Eighth and Gratiot. The south portion was an octagon built of stone and modeled after the doctor's favorite stove. The foundations were eight-feet thick, and the structure was designed to rise eight stories. However, the building was stopped at a height of 110 feet. It was seventy-five feet in diameter, and the various floors were supported by massive iron and stone columns. The center column had niches in which McDowell planned to place copper cases and bury the various members of his family. Some said the cases were designed to resemble diplomas.

Given the important role that the building would play in local history, a further description of it should be given.

> The Octagon consists of three stories. The first is designed to be a Dispensary, where the poor may come when necessary for surgical operations performed--gratuitously. The second story is a reception or faculty room and a private library room for the professors. The great anatomical amphitheatre occupies the third story. It is 75 feet in diameter and 52 feet in height. It is larger than the great amphi- theatre at Padua, which hither- to has been regarded as the largest and most beautiful in Europe. The whole is lighted by 6 large gothic windows, overlooking the seats, besides 8 skylights, 4 feet by 6 feet high, throwing their whole light directly on the central table. Around the room, and above the seats, is a gallery, where anatomical preparations, morbid specimens, paintings, etc., will be systematically arranged. The plastering is of purest white, with a cornice 7 feet wide, in gothic style, of the most massive, rich and beautiful construction. When finished, this room and its gallery will seat comfortably 2,000 pupils. Beneath the seats will be 6 large rooms for resident pupils, janitor, and for private anatomical investigations.

The northern portion of the building was brick and consisted of three stories. The first floor was a laboratory and chemistry lecture room. The second floor consisted of a common lecture room and a library. The library was similar in construction to the amphitheater and contained a fine collection of books, paintings, sculpture, specimens, etc. The third floor was devoted to a rather remarkable museum, containing among other things three thousand birds of America, minerals, fossils, anatomical specimens, and various antiquities of North and South America. It was supposedly the largest such collection on the continent. An admittance fee of twenty-five cents was charged. Medical men and clergymen were admitted free. The attic was the location of the famous dissecting room, where instruction was given each night. McDowell had invested every cent he had in this new college--$150,000. It was the most remarkable structure in the city, and because of its peculiar aspect was referred to by some as "McDowell's pepper pot."

1865 view of McDowell's Medical College.

Dr. McDowell was fervently interested in politics. Before coming to St. Louis, he had purchased fourteen hundred surplus government flint-lock muskets, at a price of $2.50 each, and three cannon, intending to equip an expedition either to go to the assistance of the Texans in their fight with Mexico, or to try to capture Northern California. Putting those schemes aside, he turned his attention to the great danger he saw overtaking the United States: the influx of various foreign groups, particularly the Roman Catholics. He generally espoused the policies of the Know-Nothing Party. He was often called upon to deliver fiery addresses. "McDowell would use any means or weapon, however questionable, in his fights and controversies. His was always a sort of guerilla-warfare of abuse and invective. This made him a much-feared foe."

To the north of the college was a large open ground parallel to Chouteau's Pond. Dr. McDowell used the area for patriotic demonstrations on the various national holidays. He would lead his students into the field, and they would fire his favorite cannon, said to have come from the pirate ship of Jean Laffite. These demonstrations not only served as patriotic gestures, but also were a reminder to McDowell's enemies what a foe he was. During such affairs, the brothers of the nearby Christian Brother's Academy cowered in fear. Some of them suspected the doctor was "a vice regnant deputy of His Satanic Majesty." How McDowell did relish his role!

Wearing a three-cornered hat of the continentals, with feathers bristling from it, having a large cavalry sabre strapped to his waist...[he] superintended the loading and firing. In loud and emphatic language he gave his orders, encouraging much cheering and telling his followers to "Make Rome howl."

Some suspected him of being an old humbug, but they couldn't be sure. Even many of his enemies had to chuckle at the antics of this completely original and uninhibited buffoon. He was like a great child playing at games. No one really knew quite what to make of him.

Dr. McDowell bore a striking resemblance to General Andrew Jackson, and made every conscious effort to model himself after the former President. He carried a brace of dueling pistols which he claimed had belonged to his hero. For added protection he had a bowie knife hanging inside his shirt. Often he would pull it out and sweep the air about him, as if to further punctuate his delightfully raucous speeches. Audiences roared with laughter and applauded wildly.

Dr. McDowell often boasted of his physical prowess and his battles with his various enemies--the Irish, Germans, and professors of St. Louis University. He was constantly issuing challenges to startled scholars and politicians to defend their views by engaging him in mortal combat. The city enjoyed laughing about these calls to action, and rarely took them seriously. Most considered them to be mere rhetoric and affectionately referred to McDowell as "Dr. Bloemieowntrumpet." Imagine the shock when in July, 1860, the news swept the city that McDowell, "That Ranting Son of Galen," had attacked the famous Frank Blair, beating him over the head with a cane. The politician had responded by "attempting to perform the Japanese disemboweling experiment" upon the doctor. Reporters rushed everywhere garnering the gory details, only to eventually learn that no such battle had ever occurred. No one could be sure how the tale had started, but most suspected the credit could be ascribed to the doctor.

McDowell had a way of twisting events to suit his ideas as to what should have happened. He believed that it was the wish of every German or Roman Catholic to have him killed. For protection the doctor always wore a brass breastplate. He also convinced the police to give him an armed escort to accompany him to and from political meetings. On one occasion the captain of the police decided to play a joke on the doctor and put his courage to the test. McDowell was speaking at the Courthouse. When he left, he expected to meet his escort. Instead, he found no one. The police captain was concealed nearby to see what the doctor would do. A student later wrote:

> He stamped his feet, walked about in all directions for half an hour or more. The night was passing and he was impatient to get home. Convinced that, by some misunderstanding, the officer would fail to keep his appointment, he determined to brave the dangers of assassination alone, and started up Market street in a brisk walk, Capt. Couzins, muffled up in his cloak, followed him. When the Doctor reach Elm on Sixth street, where the lights were getting farther apart, he left the side walk and drew his pistols; and with one in each hand, took the middle of the road. The Captain, then about twenty yards behind him also stepped to the middle of the street, and continued to follow. When the Doctor saw he was pursued he began to run. The Captain increased his pace also. About midway on the Mill Creek grade, the darkest and most dismal part of the way, Capt. Couzins fired his pistol, in the air of course. "At this," said the Captain, when afterwards relating it, "the Doctor gave a yell, and struck out like a quarter horse, and was soon out of sight."

> At the Doctor's lecture hour next morning, he entered the amphitheatre with an air of a hero who had just achieved a new victory. As was his custom before commencing his lecture, he drew his Arkansas tooth pick and two pistols, and laid them on the marble top table before him. He then told us of the blood-curdling encounter he had the night before with the emissaries of the Pope who attempted to capture him, either for torture or deportation to Rome. He said that on his way home, about midnight, having passed Spruce street a little way, on Sixth, six or eight masked assassins rushed out of the darkness and attempted to seize him. He drew his bowie knife and slashed them right and left-- illustrating with his knife how he did it. It was a terrible combat while it lasted. Two of them fell badly wounded, and were taken up and hurriedly carried away by the others. As they retreated in the darkness he fired two shots at them and had no doubt that two more of them bit the dust. The class listened to this narrative and smiled. We had heard such stories before and admired the Doctor's vivid imagination.

The students were also aware that Dr. McDowell hid under a featherbed during electrical storms and was afraid to lecture on Fridays. Often they took advantage of these fears to make the doctor the butt of their jokes.

Not all of McDowell's battles were figments of the imagination. His nocturnal visits to the various burial grounds of the city often involved him in genuinely dangerous controversies. The uncertainties of body stealing were a constant annoyance to McDowell. The problem was not so much the law (the crime was a misdemeanor) as the relatives of the deceased. Those narrow-minded individuals often became excited over the loss of a body--especially if it was mother or a sweet young sister.

On the morning of September 11, 1849, Mrs. Malter left her residence on Park Avenue, intending to visit Camp Springs, a short distance out the Manchester Road. She failed to return home. A rumor spread that her handkerchief was found near McDowell's College. Knowing the doctor's need for bodies, and his reputation as an enemy of Germans, the suspicion was entertained that the crafty doctor had lured the woman into his establishment and had dissected her. A crowd of several hundred Germans marched to Ninth and Cerre, intent upon doing great bodily harm to the doctor. As they approached, their attention was directed to the almost-completed stone octagon across the field. There they saw Dr. McDowell training his favorite cannon from an upper window.

When he gave the order to fire, the crowd broke, running in all directions. Some, in their haste to escape, plunged into Chouteau's Pond. McDowell roared with laughter. The newspapers said that it was a disgrace that the doctor could be accused of stealing bodies; McDowell agreed with the papers. Weeks later, the missing woman was discovered in Alton, quite insane. That time, McDowell was innocent. However, a tale he recorded shows just how naive the various editors had been.

McDowell learned that a German girl had died of an unusual disease. Desiring to study the corpse, he

Grave-robbers at work.

had her removed to his dissection room. The girl's family discovered that her body was missing and headed for McDowell's to reclaim her. McDowell heard that they were armed and on their way. He made haste to conceal the evidence up among the rafters. Following is his account:

> I had ascended one flight of stairs when out went my lamp. I laid down the corpse and re-struck a light. I then picked up the body, when out went my light again. I felt for another match in my pocket, when I distinctly saw my dear, old mother who had been dead these many years, standing a little distance off, beckoning to me.
>
> In the middle of the passage was a window; I saw her rise in front of it. I walked along close to the wall, with the corpse over my shoulder, and went to the top-loft and hid it. I came down in the dark, for I knew the way well; as I reached the window in the passage, there were two men talking, one had a shotgun, the other a revolver. I kept close to the wall and slid down the stairs. When I got to the dissecting room door, I looked down the stairs into the hallway: there I saw five or six men lighting a lamp. I hesitated a moment as to what I should do, as I had left my pistols in my pocket in the dissecting-room when I took the body. I looked in the room, as it was my only chance to get away, when I saw my mother standing near the table from which I had just taken the corpse. I had no light, but the halo that surrounded my mother was sufficient to enable me to see the table quite plainly.
>
> I heard the men coming up the stairs. I laid down whence I had taken the body and pulled a cloth over my face to hide it. The men came in, all of them being armed, to look at the dead. They uncovered one body,--it was that of a man, the next, a man; then they came to two women

with black hair,--the girl they were looking for had flaxen hair. Then they passed me; one man said: "Here is a fellow who died in his boots; I guess he is a fresh one."

> I laid like marble. I thought I would jump up and frighten them, but I heard a voice, soft and low, close to my ear, say "Be still, be still." The men went over the building, and finally downstairs. I waited awhile, then slipped out. At the next corner I heard three men talking; they took no notice of me, and I went home. Early in the morning I went to the college and found everything all right. We dissected the body, buried the fragments and had no further trouble.

McDowell's reputation for stealing bodies was so well established that it was said no "sophisticated" Negro would go near the college. On one occasion a Negro man was sent to collect for a bill from Dr. McDowell. In jest, the man was cautioned to avoid getting himself dissected. When the frightened man was shown into McDowell's presence, the doctor was indeed dissecting a corpse. The Negro fled in such a panic that he fell down a flight of stairs and was killed. Many Germans believed McDowell murdered the man to get the use of his body. Fortunately, there were numerous witnesses to the affair.

The worst occurrence in St. Louis resulting from this chronic fear of body stealing and dissection happened on February 25, 1844. A group of boys, playing near St. Louis University (then located on Washington Avenue), bounced a ball inside the fenced enclosure of the medical school's courtyard. When they went to retrieve their ball, the boys discovered a pit containing various parts of the human anatomy. By evening a mob of over four thousand people had assembled outside the school. A riot broke out, and the medical school was

Medical College of St. Louis University at northeast corner of Seventh and Myrtle.

destroyed. The crowd then headed for McDowell's College. The doctor and his students had quickly cleaned up their dissection room and had hidden their bodies. The mob searched the building, found nothing, and retreated. McDowell considered the whole thing a lark. His hated rivals, the Catholics of St. Louis University, had been temporarily put out of business.

On another occasion a mob threatened McDowell's College. The doctor went to the basement and released a cinnamon bear. This beast roamed out into the crowd, and they quickly dispersed. The animal was a harmless pet, but the crowd didn't know that. When the bear died, Dr. McDowell had it stuffed and placed in his museum collection.

In spite of his many eccentric habits, everyone acknowledged Dr. McDowell's skill as a surgeon and teacher. Transylvania (where he studied under Daniel Drake and graduated in 1825), in Kentucky, and the Univeristy of Pennsylvania, at Philadelphia, were proud to claim him as an alumnus. McDowell had no peer in the Mississippi Valley. His fame spread to Europe. In the realm of comparative anatomy, his knowledge was incredible. Two famous sculptors, Hiram Powers and Harriet Hosmer, studied in his dissection room. In those days before anesthetics, McDowell's skill at amputation was truly amazing; he once completed breast surgery in two minutes! However, it was also said that he was "never a close student...[and] was thorough in nothing."

Dr. McDowell was a poor businessman, kept miserable records, and was always in need of money. He would borrow from anyone foolish enough to loan him money, including his students. He rarely repaid these debts, but few seemed to have complained about this habit. He was generous in his practice, often administering to the poor free of charge. Those whom he did charge usually found that their bills corresponded to whatever was Dr. McDowell's current need.

Dr. McDowell was a renowned speaker. His wild extemporaneous talks were spiced with lurid details, language of the vilest sort, and a "jumble of sparkling wit and eloquence." A collegue said, "No man ever wagged a fouler tongue." His lectures were always well-attended, and he was constantly called upon to serve as a political speaker. He was once recognized, standing in a crowd at a Fourth-of-July celebration at Alton. He was asked to come to the stand and address the crowd on any subject he wished. This he did, choosing as his topic, "The Evils of Alcohol." He lectured several hours, occasionally pausing to take long draughts of gin from a pitcher at his side! The crowd loved it. The drunker he got, the more eloquent he became, and the more violently did he denounce imbibing!

At one of his commencement exercises, invariably held in the hall of the Mercantile Library, the doctor, playing a violin, strolled through the audience and up to the platform. He then proceeded to speak in his high-pitched voice.

Now gentlemen, we have been together five long months. Doubtless, some of these months have been very happy months, and doubtless some have been very perplexing ones. Such is the eternal fate of workers and students. But now, gentlemen, the saddest of all sad words must be uttered, namely, farewell! Here retrospection takes her sway, either gladdened or saddened, as idiosyncrasies hold the mind. We have wandered in the labyrinthian way of anatomy. We have floated in the ethereal atmosphere of physiology. We have waded knee deep, nay, neck deep, into a sea of theory and practice; ground, filtered, pounded and inspected elements of materia medica, and slowly pounded in the endless crucible of chemistry. As we say farewell! It is needless for me to say that I hope God may, in His infinite mercy, bless you as you deserve. But remember that labor omnia vincit. No man under God's blue sky need hope that success can, or will come without labor, for God has ordained that all of us must earn our living by the sweat of our brow. Nature only recognizes the laborer, and eternally damns the rich man, by satiety and disease.

Doubtless one of your number, in this class, will come back to the great city of St. Louis with the snow of many winters upon his hair and walking upon three legs instead of two, as Sphinx has it. As he wanders here and there upon its streets amidst the crowded and eager throng, noting the wondrous improvement here and the change there, suddenly gentlemen, it will occur to him to ask of one of the eager passers-by, "Where is Dr. McDowell?" "Dr. McDowell?" "Dr. McDowell?" he will say, "what Dr. McDowell?" "Why," he will tell him, "Dr. McDowell, the surgeon?" "Oh! yes, Dr. McDowell, the surgeon. Why! He lies buried close to Bellefontaine."

Slowly, gentlemen, he will wend his way thither, and there amidst the rank weeds, he will find a plain marble slab inscribed, "J. McDowell, Surgeon." While he stands there contemplating the rare virtues and eccentricities of this old man, suddenly, gentlemen, the spirit of Dr. McDowell will arise on ethereal wings and bless him, aye! thrice bless him. Then, suddenly, gentlemen, this spirit will take a swoop and as he passes McDowell's college he will drop a parting tear. But, gentlemen, when he gets to Pope's [St. Louis University] college, he will spit upon it. Yes, I say he will spit upon it.

This speech, like all others given by the good doctor, was greeted with wild applause and cheers.

Dr. McDowell's personal life was as fascinating as his other pursuits. While living in his native Lexington, Kentucky, he fell in love with his cousin, the daughter of Dr. Ephraim McDowell. The girl's father did not look with favor on such a relationship, although they were common in the South at that time. McDowell accused him of poisoning her mind against him and never ceased cursing his name. The poor girl thus missed the opportunity to have led a most interesting life.

In 1826 Dr. McDowell married Amanda Virginia Drake, the sister of his teacher, Daniel Drake. They had five sons and six daughters, but only four of these children reached maturity--Isaac Drake, John, Charles, and Anna. The three boys became doctors, and Drake and John assisted their father in the college.

McDowell's Medical School

The doctor had most peculiar ideas about burial. He designed and had built copper cases in which the bodies of his dead children were placed. The bodies were then surrounded with alcohol. One child was buried in a vault located behind the doctor's residence and college. The burial ceremony was conducted at night by the doctor. A procession of his friends and students, each carrying a torch, followed the body to the grave. Dr. McDowell bought a cave near Hannibal and suspended one of his children in a copper case, from the ceiling. When his dear wife died, he purchased one of the Indian mounds at Cahokia and built a tomb on top of it. From the upper windows of his octagon, he could spy it with his telescope. In later years these bodies were removed to Bellefontaine Cemetery.

Dr. McDowell remarried on June 20, 1856. His new bride, Sarah E. Mack, was young enough to have been his daughter. This marriage caused a split in his family, and his son Charles never forgave him. However, Drake McDowell remained his father's closest ally.

In his religious beliefs Dr. McDowell was again quite unusual. He was reared a Presbyterian, professed to be an agnostic, was fervently interested in spiritualism, and seemed superstitious to a fault. The following tale illustrates vividly his views on religion. On November 1, 1855, Dr. McDowell sat next to Reverend Artemas Bullard of the Presbyterian Church. They were aboard a Missouri Pacific train bound for Jefferson City. Bullard took advantage of the occasion to lecture the skeptical doctor on the subject of religion. Bullard so plagued him that McDowell finally jumped up, threw back his head, and announced in stentorian tones that he was going to another part of the train, adding that he believed, like sailors, that if there was a gray horse or a "damned" preacher on board a ship or a railroad train, there would be hell to pay! Bullard flushed red, while the others in the car enjoyed a good laugh. They had a short time to enjoy their joke, for just minutes after McDowell went to the rear of the train, a disaster of the first rank occurred. As they were passing over the Gasconade River, the bridge collapsed, plunging the front cars to the depths below. Many, including Artemas Bullard, were killed. Dr. McDowell, safe in a car remaining on the trestle, helped to treat the mass of wounded. McDowell's

religious metamorphosis continued, and he eventually embraced the Roman Catholic Church. His final leanings toward Catholicism seemed incredible after his having spent a lifetime denouncing that faith.

While on his deathbed he requested that he be interred, suspended from the ceiling of Mammoth Cave in Kentucky. He died September 25, 1868, at the age of sixty-three years, five months, and twenty-five days. The cause of death was a congestive chill (lobar pneumonia). Dr. John S. Moore, his former pupil and colleague, delivered a magnificent oration over the body of McDowell. The remains were then conveyed to Bellefontaine for burial. His tombstone reads:

Joseph Nash McDowell
Surgeon
1805-1868
Founder of the Missouri Medical College

The college building at Eighth and Gratiot was abandoned in the summer of 1870. A building several blocks away was selected as the new home for the medical school. For years the vacant building stood, crumbling away and looking somewhat like the ruins of a European castle; many thought the site to be haunted. The structure was demolished in the late 1870's and the property incorporated into the railroad yards which had previously spread over the dry bed once occupied by Chouteau's Pond.

For many years after the death of the old doctor, a mere mention of his name would provoke a chuckle. Yet, he will always be remembered as long as there is a medical school at Washington University. That great institution is a direct descendant of McDowell's College.

Dr. Joseph Nash McDowell

Neighbor Against Neighbor

Confusion reigned in those opening days of 1861. A decade of poor national leadership had culminated in the Union being torn asunder. St. Louis and Missouri faced the somber decision--secession or union. The vast majority of the French and American inhabitants of the city were aligned in feeling with the South. The German immigrants of the past decade were equally fervent adherents to the Union. It was apparent that any decision would bring heartbreak and despair to the divided city.

St. Louis Courthouse

On the Sunday night of January 6, 1861, a crowd of all classes packed the magnificent rotunda of the Courthouse at St. Louis to hear that august personage, Dr. Joseph Nash McDowell, present his views on the national crisis. Others tried to address the crowd, but the mulititude had ears only for McDowell.

> Dr. McDowell came up on the stand amidst deafening applause. After the excitement was allayed, he proceeded to give his views on secession; Union, compromise, and States rights. From what we could gather from his remarks, the brave old Doctor is for Union to the back-bone. He thought the Missouri Compromise line should be extended through to the Pacific Ocean. A final quietus should be placed on slavery agitation, and then all should live in peace and harmony as brothers. He thought the Abolitionists of the North had caused much trouble, but if they would mind their own business in future, and agree to compromise, he would forgive them, and allow them to live. If not, then they ought to be hung.

> The Doctor thought this vexed question could be settled. "Why will you," said he, "cut your own throats for a d——d nigger." He strongly insisted that the people of St. Louis should not cut their own throats. He had material enough (powder and shot) to prevent them from doing it. "If, however," said the Doctor, "the epitaph of this nation is ever written, it will be 'Here lies a Republic of white men, who made slaves of themselves to free a negro.' "

As spring approached, it seemed inevitable that war would come. The South opened wide its arms and welcomed some of St. Louis' finest. Dr. J. N. McDowell led the procession. At the commencement of the McDowell Medical School, February 28, 1861, the doctor delivered a farewell address to his students and faculty and announced that he was going south to offer his services to the Confederate Army. Others of Frenchtown followed his example; among them were Dr. Joseph T. Scott, who became Medical Director of the Confederate Army of the West, and P. Bauduy Garesche, who took charge of the powder works at Columbia, South Carolina. Warm wishes and a hope for a hasty return were tendered these men.

After the firing on Fort Sumter, there was intense maneuvering to take Missouri out of the Union and ally it with the Southern Confederacy. The movement had the endorsement of Governor Claiborne Jackson and much of the state leadership. State militia companies in St. Louis were ordered by the Governor to assemble on May 3, 1861. They camped for military drill in Lindell's Grove near Olive Street and Grand Avenue, naming the camp for Claiborne Jackson. Many of the Union sympathizers in St. Louis thought the force had as its intent not military drill, but the capture of the United States Arsenal in St. Louis. On the afternoon of March 10, 1861, General Nathaniel Lyon marched from the arsenal to capture Camp Jackson. His force was comprised mostly of German Homeguards of St. Louis, many of whom could not speak English. Lyon entered Camp Jackson from several directions. Stories vary as to what then happened. Shots were fired. Forty-six casualties resulted, including women and children visiting the camp. St. Louis was thrown into a panic.

Rumors circulated that the Germans of South St. Louis were preparing to march north and sack the French and American neighborhoods. Thousands fled the city. The streets were abandoned as Lyon marched his prisoners under cover of night east along Chouteau Avenue. As they passed the corner of Seventh Street, they were observed by a group of Frenchtown residents. Among the prisoners they saw their neighbors--Col. John Knapp, Mr. Leonori,

Camp Jackson

Fred Garesche', Peter Saugrain, Ed Mead, Louis Kretschmar, and others.

> We followed them as far as we could, calling "good-by" to each one recognized, and then went home to ponder on what the next day might reveal.

Brigadier-General Nathaniel Lyon

The German Homeguards moved rapidly to secure the city. They numbered five thousand and were divided into five regiments, one stationed at Soulard Market. One of their first objectives was to locate eleven hundred rifles rumored to have been shipped to St. Louis from Baton Rouge. The Germans felt these had to be kept out of the hands of Southern sympathizers, "secesh" as they were called. At the break of day, May 31, 1861, troops entered the doors of McDowell's Medical College to secure the doctor's famous private arsenal. The search produced nothing. "No arms of any kind were discovered--not even in the dissecting room." Before departing St. Louis the crafty doctor had crated his supply of arms and shipped it south, labeled as polished marble.

The Pathfinder

Major General John Charles Fremont arrived in St. Louis July 25, 1861, to assume command of the

78

Western Department. He was famous, not only as an explorer of the West, but also as the standard bearer of the Republican Party in 1856. His father-in-law had been Missouri's great senator, Thomas Hart Benton. Fremont, thought to be less rash than Nathaniel Lyon, was welcomed in St. Louis.

Fremont chose as his headquarters one of the most palatial mansions of St. Louis, the former residence of his kinsman, Colonel Joshua B. Brant, located on the south side of Chouteau Avenue, with grounds stretching from Eighth Street to Paul. The grand house, furnished in the most elegant manner and staffed by slaves, was an imperial setting worthy of Fremont's newly acquired European tastes--tastes cultivated on a recent tour of the continent. Hungarian officers staffed a private guard of three hundred men. Dressed as if for a comic opera, they staged elaborate drills throughout the neighborhood; ribald laughter greeted them at every turn.

Fremont's reign was a disaster. He had been charged with clearing all rebels from Missouri and a movement down the Mississippi against Memphis. One writer lamented:

> There was a marked lack of system in all that he undertook to do. He evidently had little talent for details; so everything in the encampments of his volunteer soldiers was in confusion. All this was inauspicious and disheartening. We had expected so much and were getting so little.

General Fremont's Headquarters, Eighth and Chouteau.

His first act, August 14, 1861, was to declare martial law in St. Louis. On August 30 the order was extended to cover all Missouri. Those bearing arms against the Union were to be shot and their slaves freed. St. Louis was in a furor. When news of the action reached Washington, D. C., President Lincoln, alarmed, ordered the proclamation rescinded. November 4, 1861, Fremont was replaced by Major General David Hunter. Fremont's career in Missouri had lasted exactly one hundred days.

To the Germans, Fremont would forever be a hero. On November 1, 1862, the German people of St. Louis presented Fremont with a beautiful sword. The occasion was turned into a spectacle such as the city had never before seen. Over thirty thousand people crowded the streets and sidewalks in front of the Brant mansion on Chouteau. The trees were filled with humanity. It was a sea of people as far as the eye could scan. Chinese lanterns were strung over the crowd. Lanterns covered the mansion and grounds. Fireworks filled the air, and Waldauer's German Band played through the night. A speech was given by Fremont to the accompaniment of Bengal Fire; he then adjourned inside the mansion to the pleasant company of a group of beautiful German ladies and a flow of champagne. The speeches continued outside until well into the night. It was a scene worthy of Fremont's Byzantine tastes.

H. W. Halleck

Major General David Hunter yielded command of the Department of Missouri to Major General H. W. Halleck on November 4, 1861, and departed for Kansas. Halleck was a robust man of forty-six and the published author of *Elements of Military Art and Science*. His assignment was to clean up the mess in St. Louis and get on with the war.

The French and American society of St. Louis was vicious in its ridicule of the Federal Army and local Germans. "The Damned Dutch" became the most popular phrase heard on the streets. Women dressed in red, white, and red--the colors of the Confederacy. Confederate flags waved from the upper stories of some houses. Women and children shouted insults at every opportunity. Fremont had had no answer to such tactics--Halleck would.

Halleck struck a decisive blow. On December 12, 1861, he issued General Orders # 24. The first section of that order read:

> The suffering families driven by rebels from Southwestern Missouri, which have already arrived here, have been supplied by voluntary contributions made by Union men. Others are on the way to arrive in a few days. These must be supplied by the charity of men known to be hostile to the Union. A list will be prepared of the names of all persons of this class who do not voluntarily furnish their quota, and a contribution will be levied on them of ten thousand dollars, in clothing, provisions, and quarters, or money in lieu thereof. This levy will be made upon the following classes of persons, in proportion to the guilt and property of each individual: 1st. Those in arms with the enemy, who have property in this city. 2d. Those who have furnished pecuniary or other enemy's service. 3d. Those who have verbally, in writing, or by publication given encouragement to insurgents and rebels.

Several leading citizens of St. Louis issued a *Protest to Maj. Gen. Halleck* strongly protesting the order. Among the Frenchtown signers of the document were Juliette B. Garesche, Robert M. Renick, Samuel Robbins, and D. Robert Barclay. They would later have reason to regret their

Maj.-Gen. John C. Fremont   Maj.-Gen. Henry W. Halleck
Maj.-Gen. John Mc A. Schofield   Maj.-Gen. William S. Rosecrans
Hon. Frank P. Blair, Jr.

public statement.

D. Robert Barclay was the first to suffer for expressing his views. A three-hundred-dollar assessment was levied against his estate, and he was branded as a "zealous secessionist." When he refused to pay the amount, soldiers from the Office of the Provost Marshal General descended upon his household at the southwest corner of Hickory and Dillon streets. They removed 250 books from his library, two book cases, and a large safe. February 18, 1862, Barclay was arrested and sent to military prison. He was charged as a secessionist. Thrown into jail with him was a city councilman. This was just the beginning of a series of arrests of prominent citizens designed to end criticism of military rule in St. Louis.

Barclay was released from prison after a stay of two months. However, his wife was arrested August 12, 1862, and charged with aiding rebel recruits to join the Southern army. The charges against her were quickly dropped. The following month the Provost Marshal General seized a row of buildings on Main Street owned by Barclay. The properties were then used to house runaway slaves. Such wanton military persecution of civilians evoked a popular lament, "The Union As It Was, And The Constitution As It Is."

No one was safe. That lioness of St. Louis society, Mrs. Tullia C. Beckwith, was declared to be a secessionist and ordered to pay a fine. A descendant of Chouteaus and Pauls, she was infuriated by the audacity of such upstart officials. Her family had built St. Louis. However, when soldiers began to empty her house of family treasures, she begged to pay the assessment. She was allowed to do so, with an added penalty. Her kinsman and neighbor, Captain Edmund W. Paul, hurled a choice epithet at the Provost Marshal; he was arrested. Another neighbor of Tullia Beckwith, Judge James R. Lackland, was carted

off to prison. The military did not bother to levy a charge against him. The writ of habeas corpus had become a memory north of Union lines.

Mr. John C. Bull lived a door or so away from Judge Lackland. Confederate prisoners were paraded past his house on April 14, 1862. A small Confederate flag was waved from his window by a girl. Other ladies in the house waved handkerchiefs and voiced their sympathies for the captured southern soldiers. The Provost Marshal then placed guards around the house and refused anyone entrance or exit. A notice was published stating that if the household exhausted its food supply, the inhabitants would be fed on army rations and treated as other prisoners.

> The same course will be pursued, we understand, towards certain other ladies in this city, unless they exhibit, a more decent regard for propriety than they have recently done.

The guard remained on duty until April 25, 1862.

The military had a difficult time coping with the wearing of red, white, and red by the ladies of St. Louis. Eventually a local wag using the title of "Uncle Sam" warned that the stated colors were the "standard advertisement of the fancy ladies of St. Louis." The writer sought to warn the ladies that they might be mistaken for what they weren't and made the subject of unwarranted solicitations. The colors were worn more than ever. The costume had become a sort of red badge of courage.

By 1862 Frenchtown had become an armed camp. The McDowell Medical School had been converted into a prison for Confederate soldiers andSouthern sympathizers. A full regiment, the Second Iowa Infantry, was quartered across the street in a row of houses on the southeast corner of Eighth and Gratiot. Camps were located at the present site of Ninth and Chouteau, near the intersection of St.

82

Gratiot Street Prison, formerly the McDowell Medical College.

Ange and Park, and at Soulard Market. A military hospital was established on Hickory Street west of Seventh, staffed by Dr. Charles H. Hughes and Dr. Melcher. Some Confederate prisoners were kept there for treatment before being shifted to the various military prisons. Government stables housing horses, mules, wagons, etc., were on the southeast corner of St. Ange and Hickory and at Eighth and Hickory. This was the largest concentration of military power in the city of St. Louis.

Banishment

On the afternoon and evening of May 5, 1863, soldiers without warning arrested twenty men and eighteen women from among the most prominent of

1841 view of the Arsenal.

the pro-Southern families of St. Louis. They were brought before the Provost Marshal and given hearings. The verdict of the court shocked St. Louis. The group was sentenced to banishment beyond Union lines. Men with families were allowed to take $1,000 each. Those without families were allowed to take $200. The remainder of their property was confiscated to be used for the care of sick and wounded Union soldiers.

The exiles were escorted from their prison cells on May 13 and conveyed under guard to the wharf. At the foot of Pine Street, they boarded the steamer, Belle Memphis. Troops formed a barrier to keep back the large crowds.

A feeling of sadness and gloom oppressed the reluctant passengers. Many of them conversed freely of their past history and prospects, enlivening their remarks occasionally with a forced jest, while others sat wrapt in silent reflection. One or two of the ladies seemed profoundly affected.

Among the list of "martyrs" were several Frenchtown residents: Daniel H. Donovan, late Superintendant of City Waterworks; Samuel H. Robbins, former member of St. Louis School Board; Dr. S. Gratz Moses (he would serve in the hospitals of Savannah, Georgia); Christen Pullis, senior member of the firm of C. & T. R. Pullis Iron Works and Foundry. Pullis' crime was that he was "a Democrat in politics, and blunt and sometimes abrupt in expressing his opinions."

The Belle Memphis reached Memphis May 15. The exiles were greeted by a large crowd at the wharf. The next morning they began a journey in ambulances and wagons, some straight from the battlefield and covered with fresh blood. For three days the prisoners went without food. At La Grange, Tennessee, a unit of Illinois cavalry took them in charge and escorted them to Holly Springs, Mississippi. That town had been so ravaged by war there were no accommodations available. They then went by train to Okolona,

The Arsenal, St. Louis, in 1866.

Mississippi, arriving there about 5:30 a.m. on May 20. At this village the weary group was turned over to Southerners. They continued by train to Columbus, Mississippi, the one major town of that state never taken by Union troops. That town, a seat of great wealth and fine mansions, gave the exiles a royal welcome. The group then rested and made plans for the future. Within a year some were allowed to return to St. Louis and take a loyalty oath. Others remained in exile until the war was over.

Few others were banished from St. Louis. Southern resistance in the city was at an end. The aristocratic families of Frenchtown and other areas had been humbled. The city settled down to an armed truce.

Gratiot Street Prison

By Christmas of 1861, McDowell's Medical College had been turned into a military prison and housed over twelve hundred inmates. The building, though not suited for prison duty, was to be employed throughout the war--"an asylum where ministrations might be made to minds diseased by rebellious thoughts." Rarely did the number of prisoners drop below three hundred, and often the number soared in excess of eight hundred. There was poor ventilation, an abundance of filth, little in the way of bath facilities, and from two hundred to three hundred men crowded into one room. Illness, particularly typhoid, was commonplace. Fortunately, prisoners were rarely kept here for any period of time. In January, 1862, a prison was completed at Alton; after a short stay at the McDowell College, prisoners were shifted to Alton. Sometimes, the vast numbers being brought to St. Louis made this impossible. Conditions awaiting prisoners at Alton

were not much better than those at Eighth and Gratiot. The Illinois prison's notorious deathrate later earned it the nickname, "Andersonville of the North."

Southern ladies made the old medical college their haunt. They brought gifts and baskets of food, and serenaded the prisoners from the street. However, during the summer of 1862, such practices were prohibited. Only sick prisoners could be visited, and then only relatives loyal to the Union. A prisoner in January, 1863, described conditions as follows:

> There are now about eight hundred prisoners in Gratiot, and more coming in every day from all parts of the country. We are allowed only two meals a day, and it keeps the cooks busy to get through with them by dark. Some two or three hundred eat at a time, and the tin plates and cups are never washed from the first to the last table. For breakfast we have one-fifth of a loaf of baker's bread, a small portion of bacon, and a tin cup of stuff they call coffee. For dinner the same amount of bread, a hunk of beef, and a pint of the water the beef was boiled in, which is called soup, and sometimes a couple of boiled potatoes--all dished up and portioned out with the hands; knives, forks and spoons not being allowed. Many leave the table as hungry as they went to it.

Runaway slaves, called contraband, were also housed in Gratiot Street Prison. They were allowed to pass out of the prison whenever they wished. They ran errands, carried water, etc. Thus, one of the easiest means of escape was to impersonate a Negro. The favorite time for escape was at dusk, just before the street lamps were lighted. At that time features, black or white, were difficult to distinguish.

B. M. Lynch, the slave dealer, fled to the South at

Jefferson Barracks

the outbreak of war, and his building at Fifth and Myrtle (now Clark) was seized and made into a prison for Confederates. When it opened in September, 1861, Max McDowell, the son of Dr. Joseph N. McDowell, was one of its first inmates. When arrested, McDowell was in St. Louis recruiting for General Sterling Price. Sanitary conditions at Myrtle Street Prison made it uninhabitable in summer; at such times its prisoners were shifted to the already-crowded Gratiot Street Prison.

Throughout the war, hopes were entertained that the two prisons of St. Louis could be closed. In the spring of 1863, a prison was rushed to completion at Jefferson Barracks; it was designed to replace Gratiot Street Prison. However, the large numbers of prisoners made it necessary to maintain all the prisons. Even though the war ended in the spring of 1865, Gratiot Street Prison remained in service until September. It was the last of the military prisons serving St. Louis.

McDowell Returns

In January, 1866, Dr. Joseph Nash McDowell

returned to St. Louis and regained possession of his famous old building at Eighth and Gratiot. During his self-imposed exile, McDowell travelled throughout Europe performing his skills in various operating theaters to great acclaim. His son, Drake McDowell, became the personal physician to the Emperor Maximilian of Mexico. Thus, it was no defeated McDowell who returned to St. Louis.

McDowell's sense of humor and boundless energy remained undaunted. He began refurbishing his old building and announced that a free clinic for the poor would soon be in service. The anatomical museum, destroyed two years before, was to be replaced. By the following month the operating theater had been replastered, painted, and papered and was again a beautiful room. One room was left as it was, and labeled "Hell." Into this chamber McDowell placed a rattlesnake, a crocodile, various statues of Satan, and a gallows from which hung an effigy of Lincoln. McDowell was very much an unreconstructed rebel.

A large crowd, comprising many students from Pope's College (St. Louis University), assembled to see McDowell's first operation since returning to St. Louis. The patient was a boy with a diseased bone in his leg. McDowell said that the child had been condemned to amputation, but "by the grace of God and the permission of Andy Johnson he would save the leg." A burst of applause swept the room, and a few tears were shed. A brilliant operation was performed. The following weeks saw similar crowds flock to see McDowell perform the magic they all expected; they were not to be disappointed. The *Missouri Democrat*, a Republican newspaper, stated: "The indomitable energy and go-aheaditiveness displayed by the old doctor in adversity stamp him as one of the most remarkable men of the age." With that remark the Civil War truly ended in St. Louis.

Other exiles and the sick and wounded came back to St. Louis. The wounds of the flesh would sometimes heal quicker than those of the memory. But, such as Dr. McDowell led the troubled city into the path of the future.

Ein Glass Bier, Bitte

The black-polished hearse, drawn by four beautifully-matched ebony-hued horses, drew to a halt at Eighth and Gratiot. John Schmidt, the driver, stepped down and surveyed the scene. It was a forbidding and frightening sight to many, and especially to a German--that giant crumbling hulk of a building, McDowell's College. "Gott in Himmel," he thought, "having to undertake such as this, burying that Antichrist himself, that bastard of a sawbones, McDowell. Why go to the

Ruins of McDowell's College.

trouble; some of his students will probably steal him back in a few hours, and who know for what dastardly purposes."

A chill travelled up Schmidt's spine as he saw the heavy doors open and the signal given that they were ready to bring out the coffin. The horses, splendidly-groomed creatures, shied and seemed to sense their master's feelings of foreboding. During the long drive to Bellefontaine, Schmidt was taxed to keep the animals under control. "Damn," he thought, "I would hate to have happen what happened to that other driver. Poor fool got caught in a hailstorm, and his horses panicked and ran away. He was thrown clear. Later, the wrecked hearse was found, but the search for the missing body was abandoned after two fruitless days. Every now and then someone still asks, 'What could have happened to that body--not the sort of thing you'd ordinarily expect people to take and not return.' Ha! If he had a mind to, I bet his lordship in the rear could tell what happened to that missing bugger."

Schmidt hurried back to Frenchtown. After caring for his animals, he made his way to Harmonia Hall to down a stein or two and have a laugh with friends. After what he had just been through, he had no wish to go home sober. A few drinks would steel him against the nightmares he had reason to expect.

The Harmonia was the working man's dream. Of all the beerhalls of Frenchtown, none other was as sordid or as popular. And of course, it was adjacent to the "notorious" establishment of Mrs. Knox. Between the two dives there were few vices or weaknesses that could not be satisfied--at least for those not overly fastidious. The corner of Park and Seventh had become a whispered promise of a good time to be had by all. And, it was in search of the fulfillment of that promise that Schmidt promptly made his way there.

The first floor of the Harmonia housed a tavern, and the noise and flow of beer were both prodigious. Upstairs was a large hall which permitted dancing as well as drinking. Some few fools took their wives to the place, but to do so was to invite insult and battle. The wise man steered clear of strangers and stayed with his regular group. Schmidt, anything but a fool, headed for his regular table. The talk there was already loud and the crowd boisterous.

"Do you remember the time those ladies attacked old lady Knox's place? What a sight! It seems some

Seventh and Park in 1884. Looking northwest.

guy went in there and blew the fifty dollars which was his life's savings. When he got home, his wife first bashes him over the head and then takes off to handle Mrs. Knox. The gals over there only laughed when she demanded her husband's money. That woman was fit to be tied. She came out in the street screaming, and then she started throwing everything not nailed down through those windows. Other good Deutsch gals heard her and dropped what they were doing to join her in battle. They charged the doors, broke them, and completely wrecked the place. Hoo! It took Mrs. Knox some time before she could get the place fit to reopen. And serves her right! What has she ever had over there worth fifty dollars?"

The talk continued loud, and the laughter lasted late into the night. Schmidt and his friends lingered for most of the evening, but most of these working men had to be up before day. Late hours were not for them.

Times were good, but the best pay most could expect to earn was a half-dollar a day. A few skilled mechanics earned a dollar a day, but those were the lucky ones. And women, well, what they earned would hardly keep a body alive. Labor was cheap, hours were long, sweatshops were the rule, and Marx was unknown. Haymarket Square was still two decades away. This was St. Louis in the late 1860's. Life was hard and bleak. What few pleasures as were available were savored and long remembered. The rich and idle were viewed as a breed apart, and only the foolish aspired to their way of life.

A German writer, new to the ways of the English language, printed a treatise presenting the lifestyle of the various economic groups among the St. Louis Germans. He could have been speaking for any of the ethnic groups who crowded the city.

There is three kinds of girles in Germany: the girle of the rich people; the servant maid, and the farmers girle.

The girle of the rich man, she goes to school like others and learns reading, writing, cheifering, and a lady teacher learns them sewing shurte, and making stokings. Sometimes gets some lessens besides until she gets confirmed. At this time begins another life for her; her parents send her to a female school one or two years and pay $50 for her this time. She is kept there like a lady, and she has not much to do. One of them has to be in the kitchen one week--another one the next week: for that she stays in the kitchen she has to take the bread in the morning when the baker comes with baskets, and the old lady showes her how to fix this and that, and in sommer time how to raise vegitables. The other time she learns playing piano and fine female work; but there is institutions where they have to work hard. Return to her parents, she stays at home until she gits chance to git married. She tries to git a preacher or a lawyer. Cannot she git one like them, at last she takes whatever she can git. Sometimes she don't marry, and lives on some interest of a little estate, because the most time there is a good many children, and there is not so much left, because an estate gets small by many parts.

But it is another case with the servant girle. After she is confirmed, she has to live out for a child's maid, because her father is a poor man and lives from his labor. He makes the capital two bets a day, and sends his daughter to live out. She gets for a full year the sum of $5.00, and one or two paares of shoes. She stays by this way in this condition a few years, and then she gits kitchen girle, and she gits $10.00 waiges for the year and at Christmas time an apron or a neke hankerchif. She has to worke hard, making the dough of the rye-bread. Some make a small dough, but big house keepings make a dough for half a dozen loafs. Every loaf wais 40 pounds. She wares wooden shoes a good many times, because the common leather shoes cost 1½ dollars. She had to do the garden work, (every family keeps her garden), takes the wheel barrow and fetch things at home along, or she carries it on her head. If she washes, she has no wash board to wash on she robbes it in her hands. She cooks the washing and takes sometimes wood ashes that hurts her fingers most into peases. Is she got so happy to get a poor laborer that makes his two bets, she helps her husband working, going out in the fields. Is her husband gits mad, he wipes her a dog. Without doing anything abainst it, she is silend like a lamb.

The farmer girle goes to school in winter time only and sommer time she has to hide the cows. She lives that way until she is confirmed. After this time she has to feed cows, hogs, chickens, and noirses the babys. After she gits strong enough, she has to thresh and go out into the fields. She git up at 2 o'cloke at neight and threshes till half-past 5, then she milks 6 cows, and goes to breakfast. For breakfast she gits a large peace of rye bread griesed with a little bit of lard or butter. At 10 o'cloke she git bread again like in the morning. At dinner time she git a peace of meat about 4 ounce havey. She eats with a wooden spoon out of a big dish with the boys. She likes a boy a marries generally one that eats with her out of the same dish and most of the time she is bound to take him. If she marries she and her husband live in a small house and pay 20 dollars a year for rent. They keep a cow and a she-goat, a little peg, make it fat and raise it, raise their own vegitables, and help other people work. He gits two bets a day, and his woman one bet a day. They are poor and never git rich.

A man can be glad to live in this

country, not minding the dole times.

But, for some life was not so hard. These were the robber barons of Frenchtown. Among the highest in this realm, ordained by God, so said the priests and Social Darwinists, were the brewers and distillers. Theirs was a society that reeked of malt and barley. They rose to such heights that their fame spread far beyong the confines of Frenchtown and St. Louis, as anyone can attest who has heard the old ditty: "First in shoes, first in booze, and last in the American League."

Almost from the beginnings of the German arrivals in St. Louis, the city became a major center of brewing and distilling. Many names would be associated with the trade, and almost all would have their roots in Frenchtown. But, as irony would have it, the first major brewery to develop in the city was that of an English family, the Wainwrights.

Joseph Wainwright, a wealthy brewer in Yorkshire, England, removed to the United States in the early 1800's, and settled at Lawrenceville, Pennsylvania, near Pittsburgh. There he owned and operated the Winterton Brewery. In 1829 Mr. Wainwright's daughter, Martha, met and fell in love with John Withnell, a recent arrival from England. Two years later, he left for St. Louis to seek his fortune in the building trade. In 1833 he returned to Pennsylvania, married Martha, and brought her to St. Louis. By the end of the decade, Withnell was a wealthy man, with such monuments as the Old Cathedral associated with his name.

Martha's brothers, Samuel and Ellis, moved to St. Louis, and by 1840 were partners in the Fulton Brewery. Samuel continued the firm after the death of his brother. In 1857 he joined with Charles A. Fritz, and their plant occupied the block bounded by Ninth, Tenth, Gratiot, and Cerre streets. Their malt house was on Stoddard (now Eleventh) between Chouteau and Hickory. Lager beer was their sole product. In 1869 the huge Fritz & Wainwright brewery was consumed in flames. The firm was rebuilt at the same site on a much grander scale. Following is an 1872 description:

The main building is 126 x 125'. It is intended to be fire-proof. The floors are covered with Egyptian roofing material, and are considered non-combustible; the partitions are all of brick. A twenty-four hourse power engine, with two boilers, each 22' long, and 40" in diameter, is employed to work the pumps and propel the necessary machinery. The mashing tub has a capacity of 240 barrels, or 480 barrels per day, when two brewings are turned off. Two brewings per day are usual during the winter season. The capacity of the boiling vat is 300 barrels. The boiling is all done by means of steam pipes, instead of the usual mode of kindling a fire under the boiler. Besides the brewery proper, Messrs. Fritz & Wainwright have a malt-house on Stoddard avenue, about the size of the brewery, where they manufacture 75,000 bushels of malt annually. Messrs. F. & W. use a large per centage of rice in brewing. It is claimed that this improves the quality and flavor of the beer.

A whole block, 300' square, is tunneled with subterranean caverns, which are divided and subdivided into convenient compartments, in which is stored the cooling beverage. There are fourteen of these artificial caverns, located about forty feet below the surface. These cellars are from 60 to 125' in length, and generally 18' high and 18' wide. The temperature in them is kept at from two to four degrees above freezing point. The present stock of beer on hand in these cellars amounts to about 22,000 barrels. Messrs. Fritz & Wainwright do not find it necessary to look beyond St. Louis for a market.

Samuel Wainwright

The firm flourished, and Wainwright became a very wealthy man. In 1866 he built a fine mansion at 1121 Morrison Avenue. He died in 1883. His widow, Catherine, a shrewd businesswoman, used much of his fortune to build the landmark still bearing their name, the Wainwright Building. That structure, erected in 1891, and designed by the great architect, Louis Sullivan, was the first of the modern skyscrapers. While the building was under construction, Mrs. Wainwright's daughter-in-law, Charlotte (wife of Ellis Wainwright) died. Mr. Sullivan was commissioned to design a tomb for her. The result is that marvel of chaste beauty in Bellefontaine Cemetery which some refer to as the Taj Mahal of America.

Ellis Wainwright assumed the leadership of the brewery. In 1883 he moved the firm to a new plant on the block bordered by Tenth, Eleventh, Gratiot, and Papin streets. Six years later, his brewery was

Wainwright tomb at Bellefontaine Cemetery.

one of about a dozen in St. Louis purchased by an English syndicate. Ellis remained as president of the newly-constituted firm until the turn of the century.

The move was then made which ruined Ellis Wainwright as a career businessman. He became a director of the St. Louis and Surburban Railway Company. In 1902, while he was out of the country, various directors of the company, including Wainwright, were indicted for bribing members of the state legislature. Wainwright lived abroad and avoided arrest. By 1911 most of the witnesses had died, and the charges were dropped. Wainwright then moved to New York City, where he lived for over a decade before returning to St. Louis to take up residence in the Buckingham Hotel. There he lived as a total recluse, hiding in other rooms when the maids had to clean. He never got over the shame of his downfall. He died November 6, 1924, and his ashes were placed in the magnificent tomb.

On August 13, 1945, the old Wainwright Brewery buildings were demolished with dynamite. Today the name is kept alive by the Louis Sullivan commissions--a lasting monument to their wealth and taste.

Scandal destroyed another giant of early St. Louis. Constantine Maguire, whose career had seemed destined for only a steady rise, fell overnight. In 1875 he was one of St. Louis' most respected citizens and the Republican candidate for Mayor. He had long been a partner in one of the most prominent drug firms in St. Louis and was the manufacturer of "Cundurango," a remedy for any ailment. This was the successor to that earlier magic elixir, "Maguire's Concentrated Extract of White Ginger":

> A valuable remedy for Dysepsia, Rheumatism, Gout, Cholera Morbus, and a preventive of Chills and Fever. It is also a powerful diffusible stimulant, and in cases of languor and lassitude, can be resorted to with success. To persons traveling upon the river, and having to drink water, unpalatable to them, this Extract will be of great service, preventing many of those derangements of the bowels which have caused fatal cases of Cholera. Those suffering with flatulency and a feeling of oppression after eating, will find great relief from its use. It possesses valuable medicinal properties, and should be in the hands of all. Price 50c per bottle.

Don't scoff at the claims for this formula. It really did cure all your ills, or so it seemed. Because, like almost all other such patent medicines of the age, it contained a hefty amount of cocaine, or a like opiate. Take a drink of the stuff and you forgot all your troubles. And, greatest of all, your addiction made you a regular customer. Yes, sad to say, most little old ladies, those who wouldn't have been caught dead letting alcohol cross their lips, took a daily swig or two from their favorite bottle of stomach medicine and then spent many happy hours rocking in a chair. The smile on their faces, which appeared to be frozen, couldn't have been removed with a hammer and chisel.

Born of Irish-Catholic immigrants, Maguire had risen from rags to riches, but the fame and the glory were shortly to evaporate. On April 6, 1875, a Democratic slate was swept to victory in the local elections. Less than a month later Maguire resigned as United States Collector of Internal Revenue. And then, the rumors began to fly. Soon after, Maguire was one of many arrested and indicted in a scandal which was to reach right to the doors of the White House. Many thought that even President Grant would fall. This was the uncovering of the great whiskey ring.

In the late 1860's there was a sizable federal revenue tax imposed on the manufacture and sale of whiskey. Almost immediately a group of St. Louisans organized to plunder and lay waste the proper collection of that tax. Mastermined by William McKee, proprietor of the *Globe-Democrat*, the group began operation as early as 1869. Their first desire was to raise campaign funds for President Grant's next race. The various distillers of St. Louis were approached and told that they should falsify records given to government officials. The records would show a certain amount of whiskey produced and sold, whereas, in reality, the amount was far greater. The tax saving would be substantial. The distillers would then make payments, from the savings they enjoyed, to the leaders of the ring. Those distillers reluctant to cooperate were told that false evidence would be used against them, and they would be forced into bankruptcy. Those who appealed to Washington for help found that no one would listen. Members of the ring boasted that they were in complete control of officials in the capital, and circumstances seemed to prove them right. In the fall of 1871, the falsification of records began. The conspiracy would involve hundreds in St. Louis.

The scam was a most lucrative one. In one year the government was defrauded of almost $1,200,000. Naturally, McKee and the leaders of the ring were reluctant to disband such a profitable operation. Grant was reelected, and business continued as usual.

As early as 1869 McKee had schemed to get Constantine Maguire appointed Collector of Internal Revenue. He finally succeeded. Maguire took office November 15, 1873. Maguire was as corrupt an individual as McKee. His moral character was known to many in St. Louis. A protest, signed by many of the city's leading citizens, was sent to Washington, but President Grant chose to ignore it. With Maguire in office, McKee had complete control of the crooked situation.

Maguire's house stood on the northwest corner of Morrison and Stoddard. Frequent were the late-night meetings held there by the various influential members of the ring. Over the months they plotted the expansion of their operation. Chicago and Milwaukee were drawn into the scheme. Eventually the operation became so big that it was impossible to keep it secret. As mumblings turned to public outcry, McKee and Maguire did not show alarm, but instead boasted that nothing would be done. Always there was the insinuation that important people in the White House knew of the affair and approved. Whenever investigators tried to uncover information, they found themselves faced with crooks who had been forewarned from Washington. Always the records and the scene seemed honest. Many thought there was no solution to the situation, and when it came it surprised all by its simplicity. The answer had been before everyone's eyes all along, and none had grasped the significance of it. True, the various distillers were falsifying reports to the government, but their bills of lading reflected the true volume of their business. In fact, the accurate accounts were being carried in the financial pages of the local newspapers!

The Secretary of the Treasury began a thorough investigation, but kept the work secret even from the President. He sent agents, posing as newspaper reporters, to the various distilleries. The cooperation was complete. They returned with all the information they needed. On May 7, 1875, the President was informed of the facts. On May 10, a raid was conducted, and the various distilleries of St. Louis were seized. On November 4, 1875, indictments were returned against McKee and Maguire, charging them with conspiracy to defraud the government. Both were found guilty and sentenced to jail. McKee was also fined ten thousand dollars. Reporters swarmed out of the courthouse and spread the news. Rumors were rampant that there was to be a general housecleaning in Washington. There were even mutterings about impeachment!

On May 17, 1876, McKee and Maguire began serving their sentences. The result was a farce. Their cells were luxuriously appointed, guests crowded in through the day, and both were allowed to slip home to spend each night in their own beds. Maguire was often reported as spending hours in a tavern near the jail. Six months after their "imprisonment" both were released. President Grant signed full pardons and remitted their fines.

The entire state of affairs was disgusting--a President seemingly oblivious to the crimes of those surrounding him; crooks who had profitted enormously and were forced to make little restitution. It was small wonder that the nation found the matter so distasteful that it was allowed to be swept under the carpet. Almost a century would pass before the presidency would again be so victimized and debased by such crooked and shallow individuals.

St. Louis is no longer home to giant distilleries. Jack Daniels packed their bags and departed long ago. Isidore Bush's marvelous winery is a thing of the past. However, beer is still big business in the city, and has been since the Germans first flocked into the town. By 1860 St. Louis was home to forty breweries. Many were quite small and flourished for a short time. Only a handful survived. Most were absorbed into the growing firms of Adam Lemp, Adolphus Busch, and Henry Griesedieck. Few remember such names as the Laurel Brewery (located on the northeast corner of Hickory and Eighth) or the Atlantic Brewery, but in their day they had small devoted followings.

The story of the Atlantic Brewery is typical of such small firms. It had its beginning in 1859. Johann Gaul built a two-story brick building at the southwest corner of Park and Hamtramck (now Thirteenth Street) and operated a modest brewery. By 1862 he devoted his time and building to the manufacture of beer kegs. Mrs. Gaul spent her time in a most interesting manner--she stole clothes. For quite some time people throughout Frenchtown complained of thefts from their clotheslines. Mrs. Gaul joined in the neighborhood denunciation of such criminal behavior. "Of course, it had to be delinquent children." But then one night, several boys saw Mrs. Gaul stealing into yards and removing wash from lines. When police searched the house, they found clothes everywhere, and of all sizes and types. Her collection was rather astonishing.

In 1864 Johann Gaul sold his brewery building to the firm of Tener & Fischer, and they reopened it under the style of the Atlantic Brewery. The following year the firm was comprised of John Fischer and Frederick Zeiner. They operated a saloon at the site and resided there. The brewery was closed in 1869, and the various members of the firm went to work for other breweries. Whatever was special about its product was lost to the world. Today, even the bottle collectors fail to recognize the name.

Constantine Schnerr's Star Brewery flourished for a decade at the southwest corner of Park and Rosatti (now Twelfth Street.) In 1869 the ten-year-old brick structure housing the brewery and saloon was purchased by Anton and Henry Griesedieck of Griesedieck & Bro. Brewery. Christian Zeiner, a brewer of rare skill and formerly with the Atlantic Brewery and later with

Schnerr, was also a part of the package purchase.

The Park Avenue site became the Griesedieck's malt house. Their brewery was always maintained at other locations. The family mansion was located immediately south of the malt house on Rosatti. A second house was constructed on Morrison. These houses were showplaces for almost three decades, and then came the tornado of 1896. Shortly after that time the Griesediecks shifted their residence to Compton Heights, and the brewery and malt house were moved further south into the area now known as Soulard. By the end of the century, this brewery was one of the three giants in St. Louis beer production. Their larger and more powerful rivals were the firms of Anheuser-Busch and Adam Lemp.

Lions guard the entrance to the Fuerbacher mansion at Twelfth and Sidney. Fuerbacher was a beer baron.

Johann Adam Lemp

errichtete vor 74 Jahren die hier im Bilde wiedergegebenen unansehnlichen Steinbauten. Dies war der Anfang der St. Louiser Brau-Industrie.

Aus diesen bescheidenen Verhältnissen entwickelte sich im Laufe der Jahre der großartige und gewaltige Betrieb der heute so vorteilhaft bekannten Lempschen Brauerei.

Auf der Panama-Pacific Internationalen Weltausstellung zu San Francisco wird die Brauerei von Lemp gut repräsentiert sein.

Das Fabrikat der **Brauerei von Lemp,** St. Louis, U.S.A.

erfreut sich einer stets zunehmenden und beneidenswerten Beliebtheit, ganz besonders

FALSTAFF,

welches ausschließlich in der Brauerei geflascht wird und dessen Ruf als ein gesundes, nahrhaftes und erfrischendes Getränk ein internationaler geworden ist.

St. Louiser und in St. Louis weilende Fremde sind stets willkommen und freundlichst ersucht, unsere Anlagen unter kundiger Führung in Augenschein zu nehmen.

The name Lemp is synonymous with great wealth and mystery. No other family of the nineteenth and early twentieth century lived in such luxury, and none other met with such tragedy. Death, like a vicious hunter, came to stalk the family. A heart attack and four suicides destroyed the dynasty and crippled a giant industry. Those who knew the answers to the family's reasons for self-destruction all lie buried in the family mausoleum at Bellefontaine.

The Lemps had everything, and much of it--wealth, looks, intelligence, and that quality so dear to St. Louisans, a sense of style. Beer running from household spigots, a monumental cave beneath the house used as a natural theater, art collected on a museum scale, great houses in the country, and the largest brewery in a brewer's town--it was all enough to stagger most observers, and onlookers there were. The Lemps were pursued by notoriety, and they played their parts beautifully.

John Adam Lemp, the founder of the local empire, introduced lager beer to St. Louis in 1838. During the next two decades his brewery grew to be the largest in the city. A splendid plant was constructed at Cherokee and Carondelet Road. Lemp was the king of the local brewers.

The Feickert-Lemp mansion in 1892.

William J. Lemp

William J. Lemp, the son and heir of Adam, married Julia Feickert, the daughter of a wealthy neighbor. At a later date they moved into her father's enormous mansion. This is the house most know today as the Lemp Mansion. William's favored child was Frederick, groomed to run the business. Frederick died at age twenty-eight of a heart attack. The Bellefontaine mausoleum, costing $60,000, was built for him. William Lemp then seemed to fall apart. He shot and killed himself in 1904. Three of his children would later resort to the same escape from life.

Prohibition spelled the end of the Lemp Brewery. The family, its sole owners, just didn't have the spirit to continue. The last of William's children, Edwin, died without issue in 1970. The old mansion

The Lemp tomb at Bellefontaine Cemetery.

on Thirteenth Street (now DeMenil Place) now does duty as a restaurant. The cave below has been sealed shut. The Lemps are gone, but they haunt the city still. A mention of their name is but the excuse for many to wax nostalgic and reminisce.

Eugene Field's poem in praise of Lemp beer is a poignant reminder of the affection St. Louis once showered upon this fabled family.

THE CHOICE OF THE GODS

The gods on high Olympus quaffed
   A nector, so historians say,
Till by some chance, one day this draught
Ran short much to the god's dismay.
"What shall we do?" old Juno roared,
Recovering from the first surprise,
No answer, save around the board
Were heard most dismal groans and sighs.
Then Bacchus cried, "I have, I think,
A treat that will excite your wonder;
I'll order up a mortal drink
That beats your nectar all to thunder."
And then to Mercury he said.
"Remember you've no time to waste,
Go glue your wings on to your head,
And off to Lemp's I pray you haste."
The gods with great impatience burned
for Bacchus' wonder to appear,
Till Mercury at last returned
A carrier of a keg of beer.
'Twas such as Lemp can only brew,
And, by the best of mortal luck,
It happened to be fresh and new,
The kind by mortals surnamed Buck
The gods consumed it with delight;

They poured libations deep and long.
Old Jupiter got beastly tight,
While Pluto sang a comic song.
They quaffed and roared and joked and spreed
With motley songs and merry laughter
And then by vote it was decreed
That Lemp should brew for them thereafter.
They banished nectar from their sight;
And ever since, from year to year,
The gods on old Olympus height
Have drunk of Lemp's refreshing beer.
It's well they do, for when they've quaffed
That fluid at their noonday session,
They find sweet solace in its draught,
And rule us mortals with discretion.

"Veni, Vidi, Vinci," Caesar's words after his conquest of Gaul, and the modest comment above the entrance to the tomb of Adolphus Busch! That Gothic pile of stone, complete with extravagant use of stained-glass and elaborate bronze doors, is the very symbol of the Busch family personality--at once lavish and gauche. What they've lacked in style, they've always disguised by a resort to spectacle.

It never hurts to marry the boss' daughter, and that is just what Adolphus Busch did. Eberhard Anheuser, the father of Lilly Busch, entered the brewery business in 1857 and soon came forth with that choicest product of the brewer's art, Budweiser. He took his son-in-law into partnership, and the firm continued as Anheuser-Busch. By the turn of the century, Busch was the giant in the St. Louis trade. Adapting to prohibition with Bevo,

Eberhard Anheuser

Adolphus Busch

Anheuser-Busch Brew House

A Bevo Fox at the Budweiser bottling plant. "Noted for their good taste."

that brew which most drinkers took to with the zeal of taking a dose of purgative, the Buschs served notice that they were not quitters. They survived and grew to be the greatest brewery in America.

To visit their plant at Broadway and Arsenal is to see a beautiful blending of past and present. Nineteenth-century structures stand beside gleaming modern buildings. Art Nouveau chandeliers vie with flourescent lights. Clydesdale horses are revered as a symbol of the company. And, it hasn't

been so many years since the German language was still being used in the plant. Busch is Frenchtown's surviving giant from the past, and it is a fitting monument to anchor that southern end of the area.

LILLIAN RUSSELL.

The Reaper Claims His Harvest

Fat, complacent, and slightly vulgar, St. Louis entered the 1890's. The decades following the Civil War had been kind to the river city. Its population had soared to a half-million, ranking the metropolis fifth in the nation. Railroads converged on that new and mammoth monstrocity, Union Station, looking somewhat like a misplaced medieval city--God, did the people love it! In an era dedicated to gluttany, the hourglass figure aside, Tony Faust's elegant restaurant hoped to please. Lillian Russell, of ample figure (those dinners with Diamond Jim) and pleasant voice (she could melt your heart), entertained in the local theaters. Local gals, hoping to be mistaken for her, doused themselves liberally with such scents as Heliotrope, Jockey Club, and New Mown Hay, and pulled the corset strings tighter. Cycling in the park was popular, and every house had to have an Emil Frei window. All who could afford to do so went to the Chicago Fair: "Did you hear what Little Egypt did?" Yes, it was a gaudy and marvelous age.

Among those of Frenchtown who enjoyed the good life were the long-established Pullis families, owners of one of the leading iron foundries of St. Louis. How could they possibly know that the end was so near.

In 1839 Christen and Thomas R. Pullis, enterprising young brothers, had come to St. Louis. They were the sons of Peter and Jane (Archibald) Pullis of New York City, and were the descendants of nobility, the Van Pullisvelts, colonial settlers from Holland. These young men were destined to become "Mechanic Princes" in St. Louis.

Christen, an excellent mechanic, served an apprenticeship in an iron foundry in New York, and afterward worked as a journeyman in the East before coming to Missouri. Along with Thomas he travelled by stage to Pittsburgh and then by steamboat to St. Louis. Immediately after arriving in St. Louis, Christen took the lead in developing an iron foundry in partnership with his brother. This was one of the pioneer firms in that line in the Mississippi Valley.

With their own lands the Pullis brothers built their plant on the west side of Sixth Street just north of Washington Avenue. They were convinced that future construction would rely more and more on architectural iron. However, they produced a variety of items including: iron railings for yard and cemetery purposes, vaults, safes, iron chairs, tables, hat racks, spittoons, umbrella stands, iron bedstands, etc.

Thomas R. Pullis

In 1854 John Pullis, another brother and a master builder, arrived from New York and joined the firm, afterward known as C. & T. R. Pullis & Bro., or the Mississippi Iron Works. Hereafter, the firm took on far more ambitious projects. In 1856 they erected a two-story brick building, including a foundry, at the southwest corner of Seventh and Hickory streets. Prior to this expansion castings were brought to St. Louis from Cincinnati. At this new site sixty men were employed, and twenty tons of metal were consumed each week. The plant was again expanded, at the same site, in 1859. That same year John built a fine house, which still stands, at 916 Hickory; this made him quite convenient to the firm. Warerooms for display and offices were maintained on Third Street near Chestnut. A local newspaper reported:

> The beauty and finish of the iron railing turned out by this establishment, had, we are all well

Iron porch made at Pullis plant in 1859.

aware, earned for this firm an enviable reputation in this city, but we are glad to learn that their reputation is also extending abroad, and that orders are arriving from distant quarters.

Thus stood the imposing firm of Pullis on the eve of the Civil War, a fledgling industrial giant--a pioneer in its field, and most of its success, to that point, could be attributed to Christen.

Christen Pullis, born in New York in February, 1815, was a born leader and a man of great integrity. He was large and of "robust health." He was a Democrat in politics, and "blunt and sometimes abrupt in expressing his opinions...[and] heartily respected for his candor and spriteness."

On November 14, 1841, he married Lydia L.

Phillips. They made their home on the east side of Seventh Street, just north of Washington Avenue, and later on the southside of St. Charles, just west of Eleventh Street. Christen's brother, Thomas R. and family, boarded at both of these addresses. In 1849 Thomas left his family in the care of Christen and headed overland for California, hoping to strike it rich in the gold fields. His wagon broke down at Westport, now Kansas City, and he walked the rest of the way. After a year of no luck, he returned to St. Louis by the water route around South America and up the Mississippi River. His sole item acquired on his journeys was a Spanish shawl which he brought to his wife, Harriet. He returned to find a family severely stricken by tragedy.

In the 1840's Christen, Thomas, and another

Pullis ironfront at Fourth and Chouteau.

brother, Peter, had all bought lands miles out on the Manchester Road. Christen built a country house, used for weekend excursions and as a residence by Peter. This country retreat became a haven during the various cholera epidemics which struck St. Louis in 1849, 1850, and again in 1851. In 1849 St. Louis lost 4,547 of its 63,000 population to that dreaded disease.

Funeral processions crowded every street. No vehicle could be seen except doctors' cabs, and coaches passing to and fro from the cemeteries, and hearses, often solitary, making their way toward their gloomy destination. The hum of trade was hushed, the levee was a desert, the streets, wont to shine with fashion and beauty, were silent. The cemeteries, homes of the dead, were the only places where there was

life, for the incessant rumblings of carriages and the tramping of feet and the murmur of voices were heard there. Physicians were kept continually on the move, on visits of mercy, going hither and thither with no hope of fee or reward, except that which might follow them to the afterworld. Some reeled through the streets like drunken men, from sheer fatigue and exhaustion.

During the three summers of plague, the Pullis family sought refuge in the country. In 1851 they were not able to outdistance the foe. Peter Pullis and Christen's wife, Lydia, came down with cholera. They were given what primitive treatments as were known--a typical one follows:

110

1129 Morrison Avenue, the "Lace House," was razed in 1946.

Ingredients--Assafoetida, opium, black pepper pulverized. These ingredients, more or less pure, will be found in every town and village.

The dose for an adult is from a grain and a half to two grains of each, made into a pill.

The best mode of administering the pill is not by swallowing it whole, lest it be rejected in that state, but by chewing it and swallowing it with the moisture of the mouth, and a very little brandy and water to wash it down.

It was all to no avail. Peter Pullis died June 28, 1851, at the age of forty-two. His sister-in-law, Lydia, died the following day. It might be noted that even the doctor who prescribed the above remedy died from cholera. The next spring the Pullis dead were removed to Bellefontaine Cemetery. Less than a month after reburying his first wife, Christen married Amelia Fargis.

Christen began to spend more and more time in the country, and in 1857 made that place his permanent residence. This property was in what is now Rock Hill and was along the north side of Manchester Road. The third tollgate west of the city limits was just east of the house. This house later burned, was rebuilt, and burned again. In 1860 Christen decided to move back to the city. He bought a townhouse at #10 Union Row, on the southside of Papin between Fourteenth and Fifteenth streets. His timing could not have been worse. To be an outspoken Democrat in St. Louis during those turbulent years of the Civil War was to invite trouble.

Christen was not just a Democrat; he was fervently devoted to the party. As the war approached, he became one of the local leaders of the Constitutional Democratic Party. When martial law was instituted in St. Louis, he spoke out loud and clear. He bitterly opposed what he considered to be violations of social decencies. His every public utterance seemed to be a denunciation of military rule. It came as little of a surprise when he was branded a secessionist and imprisoned at Alton. After a short time he was allowed to return and take a loyalty oath; it almost stuck in his throat. In May, 1863, he was again arrested and banished south of Union lines. The authorities had failed to take note that he had signed the loyalty oath; they simply regarded him as a nuisance which they wanted to be rid of. He was shipped south and ended up in Mississippi. Much of his property was seized by the military. With what little he was allowed to take with him, he opened a pipe and tobacco shop at Jackson, Mississippi. He decided to relocate at Panola, Mississippi. Enroute there he ran across Union soldiers, and they confiscated all his goods. March, 1864, found him in Mobile, "in good health, and looking very unlike a starved man." Even under the worst of circumstances, Christen never gave up. He always lived for the next day.

After the war Christen returned to St. Louis and rejoined his brothers in the iron business. His wife had kept the house on Union Row. It was a bittersweet reunion for all. The Pullis family had suffered greatly. All had been branded as secessionists and fined by the military. It was a great price they had to pay for the outspokenness of Christen.

Christen deserved a respite, but it was not to be. He soon took on that formidable foe, cholera. He was stricken at his residence on Union Row at eight a.m. August 20, 1866; he died at six p.m. of the same day. His obituary read:

He was one of our most enterprising and public spirited business men. He was a Democrat of the strictest school, and his friends, both political and personal will miss him. Those of his political enemies, who through life, have persecuted him to the sacrifice of nearly all his worldly goods, can now rest satisfied that his "frailities are over and his spirit in peace."

Following the Civil War and the death of Christen, the surviving brothers launched an intensive effort to rebuild the prosperity of their firm. They were to succeed beyond their wildest dreams. Their iron works and foundry expanded to cover the north half of the block bordered by Hickory, Seventh, Rutgers, and Eighth streets. One of their new specialties was the production of entire store fronts. Many of these still survive in St. Louis, testifying to the versatility and beauty of their product.

Due to poor health, John Pullis retired from the firm on January 1, 1874. He and his wife, Eliza Ann, later moved to Indianapolis, where his only daughter, Estelle (Mrs. Samuel A. Johnston), resided. He died February 1, 1886, in his seventy-fourth year, leaving a large fortune to his wife and daughter. His son, William W. Pullis, had died during an epileptic seizure at his home on Kennett Place on the morning of December 28, 1880. He and his wife, Jane, daughter of Firmin Desloge, had been childless. Thus ended locally the family line of a third Pullis brother. Only Thomas' family remained in St. Louis.

Thomas was now joined in business by his sons: Thomas R., Jr., Augustus, and Theodore. The style of the firm became Thomas R. Pullis & Sons. Thomas was now one of the leading business men of St. Louis. He also took an active interest in affairs of the county. In 1869 he had built a fourteen-room frame mansion on his property on Manchester Road; thereafter he made that place his home. He was a school director and was president and organizer of Oak Hill Cemetery Association in Kirkwood. He died at his country home August 29,

1878, and was buried at Bellefontaine.

The firm then became Pullis Brother's Iron Company, with a capital stock of $200,000, all held in the family. Theodore died January 2, 1884, leaving the business in the control of his two brothers. By 1887 the foundry employed over two hundred men and shipped to every state in the West and South and to Mexico. The warerooms and offices occupied two fine three-story buildings at 206 and 208 North Sixth Street.

Early in 1892 an immense trade outlet was opened in Chicago, necessitating that a branch be located there. Thomas R., Jr., moved to Chicago to head that office, leaving the booming foundry and St. Louis office in the charge of Augustus. Augustus died in November, 1894, forcing Thomas to return to St. Louis to manage the business alone. Pullis was then one of the most famous names in the Midwest, and the firm was on the verge of further expansion. The year was 1896, and the future seemed bright.

During the Gay Nineties, Harriet, the widow of Thomas R., Sr., had moved to a beautiful mansion on Waverly Place, by then far more fashionable than the older neighborhoods of Frenchtown. European trips, lavish parties, the best of clothes and jewelry, had become commonplace to this favored family. All the tragedies of the past had been forgotten. The family was rising to giddy heights on the boom of the nineties. Their carefree lifestyle typified that gay decade.

Shortly before five o'clock on the afternoon of Wednesday, May 27, 1896, the servants of the Pullis household were busy preparing dinner. Suddenly, a sound began, somewhat resembling the noise made by a long train going through a tunnel. And then all hell broke loose! The sound of breaking glass and timbers snapping, combined with the roar of an eighty-mile-per-hour wind, was deafening. After a few moments there was silence, and then screams, and then came the blinding rain. The clouded view from the windows down Waverly Place revealed an impressionist nightmare of destruction and confusion.

A terrible tornado, the worst that had ever hit St. Louis, touched down west of Shaw's Garden. At Grand, between Lafayette and Shenandoah, that funnel merged with two others, and they moved in a single wide path of destruction across Compton Heights and Lafayette Square. East through Frenchtown the terrible storm swept, lavishing its worst attention upon those crowded neighborhoods that had stood for a half-century or more. The *Globe-Democrat* reported:

> That the dead are not 1,000 and the wounded 10,000 is the mystery after one has threaded this part of the storm cloud's path. "Where is the worst" one is asked. That is hard to tell, but certainly there is nothing worse than can be witnessed from Lafayette Park northeast to Broadway, a long mile. It is desolation....There are streets which can not be traversed because of the debris. There are a thousand windows smashed, whole rows flattened to the ground, street cars overturned and wrecked....Up and down Broadway, from Chouteau avenue for a quarter of a mile each way, the storm has wrecked the stores....From Broadway to the river, through the oldest part of St. Louis....is a long record of wrecks of buildings that were entitled to historical tablets.

Night descended rapidly, enveloping the destruction in a shroud of darkness. All municipal lights were extinguished. Moans were heard everywhere. People sat drenched in roofless houses gazing at the stars which were starting to shine. Working husbands toiled for hours through the streets filled with rubble, afraid of what they would find when they got home.

The wreckage revealed the next day was worse than most had first imagined. The deathtoll reached 306, and Frenchtown had its ample share. The intersection of Seventh and Rutgers streets had disappeared into a pile of rubble. No other spot in the city saw such total devastation. Days later bodies were excavated at that corner, the total finally reaching twelve. The beautiful Soulard mansion at Twelfth and Lafayette, St. John Nepomuk, the Church of the Annunciation, Walther College, Soulard Market--all were gone. And everywhere there was the sound of hammering, as the living went about clearing the debris and repairing the damage, sometimes under macabre circumstances.

> At St. Vincent de Paul's one priest stood on the shattered roof and directed the work of the repairers, while his associate said the offices for the dead, as one body after another was brought in for the rites. The hammers of the carpenters above drowned at times the chant of the mourners below. The incense from the swinging censer enveloped the casket and mounted upward to the nostrils of the busy roof repairers and mingled with the smell· of the smoking tar.
>
> "Whose funeral is it?" was asked of a hurrying workman at the church door.
>
> "I don't know," he replied, "but there is another coming right away."
>
> The bearers lifted the casket and followed the priest down the aisle. The little group of mourners followed. As the cortege moved off from the church door another came. And all of the time the work of repair went on.

Among those waiting at the steps of the damaged church was the venerable John Schmidt, in his

114

thirty-fifth year as a hearse driver, and for the last twenty-eight years employed by Adolph Meyer at Seventh and Park. Early that morning he had walked the short distance from his home at 922 Hickory to the funeral parlor and livery stable. Pulling up to the church, he had quickly realized that this catastrophe approached in scope the great cholera epidemic of 1866. Then he had buried from two to four victims every night. Like then, the tornado had produced a hearse famine. The dead were being carried away in wagons and delivery vehicles. Amidst such confusion Schmidt stood as a pose of elegance, calm and collected. His beautiful team and polished hearse seemed curiously out of place in all the rubble and babble of mourners.

Immediately after the tornado struck, Thomas Pullis had made his way through the debris to Waverly Place. There he wept at finding his family safe. Then through the darkness and confusion he threaded a path to Hickory Street. As he went along, his spirits were given a boost when he saw the old house of his Uncle John, damaged but still standing. Another block and he stopped, gazed for a time, and turned away. The massive Pullis Iron Works was a total wreck. At a quick glance it was obvious that little could be saved. Almost sixty years of labor had been swept away in seconds, and there was no insurance. A broken man returned home.

Broadway, the morning after the 1896 tornado. The view is north from Barry.

(*Above*) Sts. Peter and Paul Church.
(*Below*) St. Paul Church. Ninth and Lafayette.

(*Above*) Bohemian Gymnasium, Ninth and Allen.
(*Below*) City Hospital. Twelfth and Lafayette.

(*Above*) Eighth Street near Rutgers. Looking south.
(*Below*) Soulard and Seventh streets.

(*Above*) Eighth and Rutgers. Looking east.
(*Below*) Annunciation Church. Built at Sixth and LaSalle in 1860.

One of the beneficiaries of the 1896 tornado, northwest corner of Seventh and Lafayette.

In later years descendants would argue over what then happened: Thomas was unable to cope with the staggering task of rebuilding; Thomas could get little cooperation from his sons--they were content with their lot; the acceptance of the tempting offer from the rival firm of Christopher Simpson, for what remained of the machinery, was a tragic mistake. Probably all of these had their share in the further decline of the Pullis fortune. Some say Thomas died of a broken heart.

Frenchtown, like the Pullis family, was never again the same. The damage had been too massive; the memories were too tragic. For most, it was just easier to move away and try to forget. The century was drawing to a close. Those who pondered probably thought:"Well, the French left a long time ago, and now go the Germans. I wonder who will follow next." Long after the vans rolled away from the wreckage, the sound of the hammering continued.

Sauerkraut, Gemütlichkeit and The Katzenjammer Kids

"But Mother, I don't want to go to Uncle Ernst's house. I want to go home and find out what's happened to my goat."

"Still Liebchen! This is an important day. Everyone will be there. And later we will go to the park for the celebration."

"There you go again! Mother, it's so embarrassing when you use German in public. Don't you know the other children in the neighborhood make fun of you when you talk like that?"

"Not speak German when I want to! Why, I'll have you know that you could once walk from Chouteau Avenue south to Arsenal Street and hardly hear a word spoken that was not German!"

"I know, Mother. I've heard you say that before. But this is May 27, 1914, and those days are past. Hardly anyone speaks German anymore, except the older people. Don't you understand?"

"Wait until I tell your Uncle Ernst. He will have a talk with you. Now, pick up your ball and straighten your hat. Pull your knickers down. We are almost there. My, but it is going to be hot today."

"D——d hot," came a voice from nearby.

"Don't mind him, Madam," spoke a quiet gentleman across the aisle. "This younger generation doesn't know how to talk in front of a lady."

"Thank you, Sir, but I wasn't offended. I'm afraid it will be far hotter than he said. Come Liebchen, and be careful. You know how dangerous it can be getting off the streetcar."

"Oh, Mother! Why do we have to come down here? None of the family lives around here any more, only Uncle Ernst. Why can't he move nearer to us?"

"Uncle Ernst likes it here. Frenchtown is his home. He has lived here most of his life. Clem, be especially nice today, for this day is special. You know, I told you."

Just at that moment they turned into the small yard and went up the limestone steps to 1115 Rutgers Street. The two-story brick with its frame mansard was an impressive structure, set in a row of look-alikes, and a mirror image of the houses on the south side of the street--narrow dark passages separating the various buildings. Clem was thinking how it was the perfect neighborhood for playing hide-and-seek. And then came the voice of Aunt Ida as the heavy wooden storm doors sprang open.

"Come on in and get out of the heat. Uncle Ernst is upstairs in his study looking over the notes for his speech. Run up and greet him, Clem."

Ernst Olshausen

"He's being impossible today. All he can think about is that missing goat of his. Gehen Sie Liebchen! Go see your Uncle Ernst."

The child plodded up the stairs and paused in the hall. He could see the erect figure of his uncle sitting at his desk, carefully pouring over his speech. It was a familiar sight. It seemed as if every time Clem had seen Uncle Ernst, he was either writing or editing something.

"Hello, Uncle Ernst."

"Why Clem, come in, child. Give your uncle a great big hug."

Just then a whistle came from the speaking tube. Uncle Ernst lifted the plug and placed his ear near the pipe. He listened for a few minutes and turned back to the child.

View east from Ernst Olshausen's window at 1115 Rutgers.

Backyard of Olshausen residence at 916 Hickory. Arthur Olshausen Sr. and wife.

"It looks as if I've got to make two speeches today. Your mother says you preferred to stay home. Don't you know what is going to happen today? Hasn't anyone told you what we are commemorating?"

"Well, I know it has something to do with an old statue."

"Enough! You do need to be spoken to, especially after what I just heard from your mother. Is it true that you are embarrassed to speak German in public? Clem, never once be anything other than proud of your German heritage. Why, you know it was our people who made St. Louis what it is today. When we came here, this was just a frontier town. The schools, the theaters, the parks--all of them reflect the work of Germans, and don't you forget

it! If your Grandfather Arthur heard you speaking ill of the German language! Gott in Himmel! Why, for ages this family has been in the newspaper business, and the German-language newspaper business at that! Why child, that is what this whole day is about! Now go downstairs and tell everyone that I will be down shortly. Have the car brought around so that we can be off."

Once again it was hat-and-knicker-straightening time. As they headed out to the car, Helga called from the kitchen that dinner would be ready when they returned.

The short ride to Reservoir Park seemed over almost before it began. Crowds of people stood back to allow the Olshausen family room to alight from

The Naked Truth. Located in Compton Reservoir Park.

the car. The huge water tower caught Clem's eye. The mammoth structure loomed over the park, dwarfing the huge mansions across the street. Near the northwest entrance of the park, a platform had been built and draped with bunting. Nearby drapery covered a large object--the statue. The band was tuning and getting ready for the occasion. The crowd was slowly assembling throughout the park. Uncle Ernst led his family to a place of honor on the platform.

"How long are we going to be here? I want to go and look for my goat. Mother, are you sure Father didn't sell him? I don't see why he had to get so mad. Fritz didn't butt him that hard."

Just then the band struck up a martial air. A large limosine had just pulled into the park. Everyone recognized it as the Busch's car. It was going to be such a grand occasion. Everyone who was anybody in the German community had turned out for the affair.

And then the speeches began. Several orators rose, spoke for long periods of time, and then sat down. And then it was time for Uncle Ernst to address the crowd. He walked to the fore, turned and gazed for a moment at his adoring family, and turned once more to the crowd. Clem stirred nervously, only listening occasionally, mostly daydreaming or staring at the draped figure that was the subject of all this commotion. The warm sun caused him to dose, and he only heard bits and pieces of Uncle Ernst's speech.

"My friends and fellow-citizens of St. Louis, we are gathered here today to honor the German press of St. Louis, and in particular the memory of three men--Preetorius, Schurz, and Daenzer. But, in a larger sense we are here to pay honor to the German heritage of this city.... and it was just seventy-seven years ago that my father, Arthur Olshausen, came to St. Louis from Holstein. After serving a short time as typesetter, he purchased a

partnership in the *Anzeiger des Westens*. In 1847 he became the sole proprietor.... After a decade of little competition, he saw Daenzer create the *Westliche Post*.... In 1860 my uncle, Theodore Olshausen, formerly a lawyer, journalist, and member of the provisional government of Holstein, came to St. Louis and purchased the *Westliche Post*. As editor-in-chief, he led the paper through the turbulent years of the Civil War, always supporting the Union. Afterwards, his health failing, he sold the paper to Emil Preetorius and returned to Germany."

"In the late 1860's my father, Arthur Olshausen, joined in partnership with Preetorius and Theodore Plate to continue publication of the *Westliche Post*.... and as you know, such celebrated writers as Carl Schurz and Joseph Pulitzer worked for and were trained by these famous publishers. I well remember many occasions when these men gathered at our house, at what was then 916 Hickory. The conversation was of national importance. They helped to shape the destiny of America...."

"And so we gather here today to dedicate this statue. I am told that the torches on either side of the monument represent the enlightenment of Germany and the United States...."

Clem was suddenly aware that his uncle had finished speaking. A pretty lady pulled the cord and released the drapery from the statue. The material floated to the ground revealing a huge naked female figure. First there was a stunned silence, then a muttering, and finally an uproar. "Have you ever seen anything so scandalous?" "I think they ought to call it the Naked Truth." "There must be a mistake!" Clem turned to see what everyone was talking about. He thought he saw something interesting, but he couldn't be sure. His mother's hands clasped themselves around his eyes so rapidly that he was almost dazed. He felt himself

Westliche Post staff about 1878. Left to right: Schnake, Gus Olshausen, Carl Schurz, Arthur Olshausen Sr., Emil Preetorius, Ernst Olshausen, Gaston————, E. Todt, P. O. Grieb, Mueller, Tenie, J. Krueger, Arthur Olshausen Jr., O. Hilpert, F. Wolf, O. Olshausen, Oscar Hoefer.

Carl Daenzer   Emil Preetorius   Carl Schurz

Anzeiger des Westens

Westliche Post

House with small balcony is Arthur Olshausen residence at 916 Hickory (old numbering system). Now demolished.

being tugged to the waiting car. Only when they were inside did his mother release her grip.

"But, I thought we came to see the statue? Why can't I go back and see it? Why is everyone so quiet? I want to see the statue!"

The strained silence of the family, further emphasized by the persistent questions of the child, continued until they returned to 1115 Rutgers. Once inside they seated themselves in the parlor. Helga, hearing their early return, came to tell them that dinner would not be ready for awhile. Uncle Ernst told her that it was all right. Besides, he felt the family could all do with a glass of sherry before dinner.

Everyone took a seat in the large parlor. Uncle Ernst broke the silence by announcing that it was time Clem was told a few things about the Germans, Frenchtown, and the family.

"Do you realize that Germany is the most powerful nation on the face of the earth? Her scholars stand in the forefront of all fields. Always be proud that you are a German."

"Be quiet, Ernst," spoke up Aunt Ida. "The boy heard enough of such talk at the cermonies. I think that it is time he learned something of the family. Clem, all your family once lived in this immediate vicinity. Your Grandfather Olshausen and his children lived in houses over on Hickory Street. That is also where my father, George Weinhagen, resided. Our old house was at 928 Hickory. Father was in business with his brother-in-law, Julius Hunicke. They had a malt company in the 1100 block of Lavielle, which you know as South Twelfth Street. Your Uncle Julius also owned a mineral water company located on the northeast corner of Twelfth and Hickory. How he ever found time to

128

serve as a Police Commissioner of St. Louis I will never know. My Uncle William Hunicke was a very successful commission merchant and was President of the St. Louis Floating Dock & Insurance Company. He was also the first treasurer of the Germania Club."

"What was the Germania Club, Aunt Ida?"

"Liebchen, it was the great hall where everyone in society went to dance and be entertained. It was a beautiful ballroom and auditorium attached to the rear of the fine old Harrison mansion. Unfortunately the tornado wrecked the structure. Why, when Waldauer's orchestra played there, the place seemed as if enchanted. Mr. Waldauer, what a remarkable man! Clem, he was one of the founders of our symphony, and he lived at Ninth and LaSalle. Ernst, do you remember that play of his which I enjoyed so much, the "Organ Grinder"? My, I haven't thought of that in years. And something else I haven't thought of for so long. Ernst, do you remember Champagne Unger's house on the southeast corner of Seventh and Chouteau? Every winter his windows were filled with the most beautiful hyacinths in St. Louis. But enough, I was telling you of the family."

"Uncle William's family lived at 1016 Morrison Avenue. His wife was the daughter of the German consul. Their home was one of the social centers of the German community. And then there was my Uncle Henry August Hunicke who lived at 922 Morrison. He had the finest hat and cap business in St. Louis. And you certainly know your family, the Hartmanns. They also used to live in this area.

Germania Club. Formerly the James Harrison mansion.

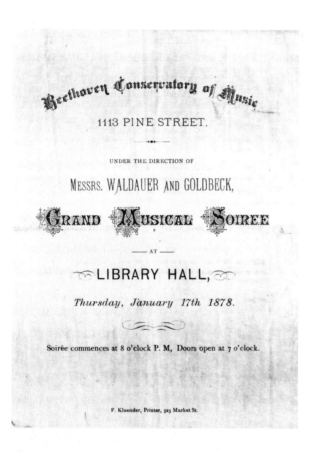

Beethoven Conservatory of Music

1113 PINE STREET.

UNDER THE DIRECTION OF

MESSRS. WALDAUER AND GOLDBECK,

Grand Musical Soiree

— AT —

LIBRARY HALL,

Thursday, January 17th 1878.

Soirée commences at 8 o'clock P. M, Doors open at 7 o'clock.

F. Kluender, Printer, 323 Market St.

Baby Ruth Hartmann in fall of 1908.

Clem, it was so wonderful. We visited back and forth. It was a rare day when some member of the family did not drop in."

"There are so many stories that we could tell you, some of them quite amusing." She reached down to pick up a strange square of material from a table by her chair. "Do you know what this is? It is a piece of an elephant which the Hartmann Hide Company tanned for the St. Louis World's Fair. The hide attracted almost as much attention as the Igorote Village."

"What was the Igorote Village, Aunt Ida?"

"Ida, wasn't that that primitive tribe from the Far East who wore no clothes and ate dogs?"

"That's enough, Ernst, we will change the subject."

"I'd like to know more about the Igorotes."

"Ida, why don't you tell him about the Hartmann who ran away with the wet nurse and was found months later stirring a pot of glue in a cave outside Denver?"

"Ernst! I do believe you have had too much sherry! Clem doesn't want to hear such tales."

"Yes I do, Aunt Ida!"

"Still, Clem!"

"I never get to hear about anything interesting. You folks wouldn't even let me get a good look at the statue. I hope someone has found my goat. Mother, are we going home right after dinner? I want to look for Fritz."

"Ida, can't you see that you are boring the boy? Let me talk for a few minutes. I think we have all heard enough about family. Clem, not only were we once close to the family that lived in this area; we were close to all our German neighbors. The entire area was like one great family. When someone needed help, he had only to ask, and people came to his aid. And it was all so informal. In summer men even wandered around in shirt-sleeves, sometimes even without a vest or tie."

130

"The area was so quiet that you could hear a keg being tapped a half-block away. At such times the hammer and shears were put aside, and every man in the area descended upon his neighbor's house for a bit of hospitality. Maybe you would just walk down to a corner tavern for a slice of roast beef, some bread, and a glass of beer. And Sundays, they were marvelous. There was a regular migration to the parks and gardens. Everyone you hadn't seen during the week you saw on Sundays. Our American neighbors thought this a desecration of the Sabbath, but we gradually won them over. And the food! Clem, it was incredible. I well remember a wedding Ida and I attended. Ida, hand me my scrapbook! I would like to read to Clem the newspaper account of the food. Let me see now. Here it is."

Wealthy German Wedding a few days since--food consumed-- 5 loaves Switzer Kase (cheese), 1 bbl. sauer kraut; 27 kegs bier; 16 gallons coffee; 69 chickens--27 roasted, 42 boiled in soup 10 geese; 2 calves; 4 hogs; half an ox; 24 hams; 1 bbl. wine; 18 gallons whisky; bread of 4 bbls. flour; cakes and pies of half barrell flour. 75 families present. Of course great hilarity prevailed; and we are permitted to state that the company didn't go home till morning, and that there was nothing to eat when they left.

Eighth Street south of Soulard. View is to the north.

Liederkranz Hall. Southeast corner of Thirteenth and Chouteau.

Ballroom of the Liederkranz. This lavish ballroom was often the scene of grand entertainments for the German populace of St. Louis. Built in 1880, the structure was demolished in 1957 for the second phase of the Darst Apartment project.

Costumes worn at the 24th Annual Carnival at the Liederkranz Club on the night of
January 26, 1895. Revelers spent fortunes on their elaborate dresses. Costume
on left represented the flower girl, that on the right, the peasant girl.

"Uncle Ernst, hearing about all that food has made me hungry. Can't I go and see if Helga has dinner ready?"

"Just a minute, Clem. I want to tell you one more story. It is about a little boy like you. Years ago, just after the Civil War, the Vogel family, whom you may know lives over at 715 Hickory Street, resided on Soulard Street. Young Guido Vogel was out in the yard, dressed in a Civil War uniform, playing with his toys. Some gypsies came by and stole him and took him to Illinois. He was such an ornery little cuss that they abandoned him in a field. His father, Benjamin, a prominent orchestra leader, was brought the news just as he was about to begin a concert. The poor man's hair turned white overnight."

"Days later, a Negro was hunting in the Illinois marshland. His dog scented something and went right to the sleeping child. The Negro turned the boy over to a white family who lived nearby. A day or so later the man of the household had business which took him to Mr. Vogel's piano store. While in the store, he was telling a customer about the lost child. Mr. Vogel overheard and asked to accompany the gentleman home. Thus was Guido Vogel reclaimed. He now has his own orchestra."

"Mr. Vogel purchased that dog from the Negro, and it was pampered for the rest of its life. The Vogels still keep a portrait of that dog in their parlor. Now, wasn't that a fascinating story? Yes Clem, this was a wonderful place to live. And though most of my friends have moved away, I still enjoy living here."

Helga then announced that dinner was ready. The family made their way to the dining room and were seated. The table was set with the finest china, crystal, and silverware, for this was a day planned to be remembered. A sumptuous feast was being spread--so much of everything. And that huge covered waiter. Clem could hardly wait to see what it concealed. He was happy and animated. The cover was lifted, and a marvelous aroma arose from the roasted carcass. Just then a scream of anguish was heard. Tears formed in Clem's eyes. He would never forget this day. There on the huge waiter was a roasted goat.

"Oh Fritz!"

Emma Lazarus' Children

In the nineteenth and early twentieth centuries, the Germans dominated in Frenchtown, but several other ethnic groups carved out enclaves for themselves in the area. The earliest and most numerous of these nationalities were the Czechs, or Bohemians. They were to be followed by the Lebanese and the Croatians. They are the unsung immigrants of St. Louis. Upon arrival, they were not as well-educated or as wealthy as their German neighbors. They did not possess the numbers to make themselves politically powerful. It was many years before they rose to positions of importance, and for most this came after departing their neighborhoods in Frenchtown.

Bohemian Hill

The political upheavals of 1848 which sent the masses of Germans to America also propelled numerous Czechs from their province of Bohemia. That very year saw the first of a steady immigration begin to pour into St. Louis. These people were quick to settle near the intersection of what is now Ninth and Lafayette, and the surrounding area took the nickname of Bohemian Hill. By 1854 the population was large enough to organize its own church, St. John Nepomuk, the first Czech church outside Bohemia. A frame building was erected at Eleventh and Lafayette. A school was soon added to serve the needs of the community.

Most of these settlers were laborers, and they found ready employment in the factories of Frenchtown. Adolphus Meier's huge cotton factory, the first west of the Mississippi River, stood nearby at Menard and Soulard. This plant was in reality a sweatshop working almost exclusively boys and girls. Laclede's Flour Mill at Ninth and Soulard worked almost exclusively Czechs. Industries of the day, like neighborhoods and churches, centered about certain national groups. Language differences made this necessary.

Several Czech language newspapers sprang up and flourished for short periods. The first of these was the *Narodni Noviny*, published by Joseph Erban in 1860. From 1863 to 1867, *Pozor Americaky* served Bohemia Hill. Its name was then changed to *Obcanske Listy*, and it survived another five years.

The most prominent of the nineteenth-century Czechs of St. Louis had no affiliation with St. John

St. John Nepomuk Church

Nepomuk, for he was the famous Jew, Isidore Bush--intellectual and businessman of the first rank. Son of a wealthy printer and publisher, Jacob T. Bush, he was born in Prague on January 15, 1822. He received the finest of educations, learning to speak fluently four languages. He could read and write Greek, Latin, and Hebrew. Like many other liberal thinkers, he fled Europe in 1849 and came to the United States. The following year he arrived in St. Louis.

He quickly established himself in the grocery business, later hardware (Bush & Taussig at Broadway and Park), and by 1853 was President of the People's Bank. Bush, an expert in life insurance matters, became an officer of the German Mutual Life Insurance Company of St. Louis. He served on the City Council and the School Board. He was fervently interested in politics and was important at the local and state levels. He was truly a tremendous asset to St. Louis.

His residence was first on the west side of Seventh between Hickory and Rutgers, but in 1859 he built a two-and-a-half-story brick house on Fulton Street between Marion and Barry. It was many years later that he moved to his final residence at 1311 South Thirteenth Street.

After 1865 Bush achieved world fame. That year he organized the International Bank, along with F. S. Beherns and August Liesse, all residents of Frenchtown. But, it was also that year that he went into the grape culture. In Jefferson County, at Bushberg, he planted a huge nursery and vineyard.

1037 Morrison. Henry Clay Pierce home in 1870. Mrs. Esther Sakowsky's grocery in 1930. Morris Fanzer's grocery in 1940.

Within a decade his wines were the talk of France and Germany. In those days when Missouri was the leading wine-producing state in America, Bush was king of the heap. People came from everywhere to inspect his grand champagne depot and arched wine cellars.

Bush died August 5, 1898. Businessman, writer (a published history of the Jews of St. Louis), politician--he excelled as each, truly a man for all seasons.

Other Czechs centered their alignments outside the structure of the parish of St. John Nepomuk. The anti-clerical Cesko-Slovansky Podpowjici Spolek, a fraternal-benevolent insurance society, was organized at Jacob Mottl's saloon and boarding house on Ninth between Soulard and Lafayette. In 1871 a Bohemian National Hall was built at Ninth and Allen to house secular societies.

The Czech community continued to grow throughout the nineteenth century. Just as German was the language of surrounding neighborhoods, Czech was heard everywhere from Park Avenue south to Allen. By the late 1890's St. John Nepomuk had over one thousand families affiliated with it. A second church, St. Wenceslaus, was built at Oregon and Arsenal in 1895. Then came the tornado of 1896. The area of Bohemia Hill was severely damaged. St. John Nepomuk was demolished. Houses everywhere lay in ruins.

The area quickly rebounded. A new St. John Nepomuk, similar to the old church, but larger, was built. The houses were repaired, and by the turn of the century over seven thousand Czechs called the area home. For over two more decades the area remained a flourishing ethnic neighborhood, but the 1920's brought changes to Bohemia Hill as it did to the rest of American society. The automobile and changing attitudes concerning family and lifestyle caused a gradual dispersal of the Czech community, only slowed by the economic rigors of the great depression. After World War II the process was accellerated. The construction of the Third Street Expressway and the nearby Darst-Webbe-Peabody Housing Project sounded the death knell of the neighborhood. Today, Bohemia Hill is a fading memory.

Children Of The Levant

They sprang upon the local scene with a color and panache unequalled by any others, these children of the Levant. They were the descendants of those fabled settlers of Tyre, Byblos, and Sidon--the Phoenicians. Creators of the alphabet, and traders such as had no rivals, their cedar and purple dyes had been sought by potentates from Solomon to the Caesars. Carthage, their offspring city, once had vied for leadership of the very western world. Antioch, in its day, was one of the four great cities of the Roman Empire. Yes, theirs was a heritage such as few others could claim.

The seventh century saw earthquakes and a Moslem host sweep across the Lebanon. For centuries afterward the land was caught in the struggle between the followers of the Prophet and those masters of deceit and splendid pastimes, the Eastern Romans, or Byzantines. The Christians of the land, formerly adherents of the Archbishop of Antioch, sought refuge in the mountain valleys and remained there until the nineteenth century. Then lured by those sirens, the Greek promoters of emigration, they came down to the coast and took to the sea as had their ancestors, and sailed beyond the Pillars of Hercules.

The first of these Lebanese arrived in the United States in 1853 and in St. Louis in 1856. Their colorful dress and Arabic language set them apart. Their exotic music and food were unlike anything the local citizenry had ever been exposed to. Few learned to know them, because of their small numbers. The flow of immigrants was only a trickle for the next four decades, and then came the 1890's.

Changes in immigration laws opened wide the doors to the East. By the turn of the century, a small Lebanese colony, known as "Little Syria," was forming just south of the downtown business district, centering on Second, Fourth, and Broadway. On October 19, 1898, the Church of St. Anthony the Abbot was organized to serve the community of fifty families. An account, published in February, 1900, described the neighborhood:

> At the corner of Second and Plum there stands a row of old two-story houses, which by their appearance indicates the fact that they are the homes of the very poor. The ground floor is occupied by the humblest class of shops, the front room being, in most cases, devoted to stocks of goods, probably not exceeding $50 in value, while the rear rooms on the street level are occupied by the family of the owner. The man of the family usually has some employment which takes him away from home during the daylight hours, so his wife waits on the few customers who drop in, attends to her household duties and manages the large family, which seems to be the inevitable burden of the poor man's life.
>
> The entrances to the second story are from a paved yard in the rear, three or four flights of wooden stairs leading directly from the yard to the rooms above. At the third flight, a white cross painted on the red brick wall indicates the location of what is probably the most curious place of worship in the city [located at 618 South Second Street]. As the visitor enters from the porch he passes first into a little vestibule. On his right there is a small confessional, with a green baize curtain, to protect from curious eyes the person who is making a confession. On the left

> a small china basin, not much larger than a match box, hangs on the wall, the receptacle for holy water. Turning toward the west, the visitor faces the altar, a small but tasteful structure, perfectly decorated with candle sticks, vases of artificial flowers and other ornaments, and above it, on the wall of the Second street front, hangs a large picture of the patron saint of the place, St. Anthony the Hermit, sometimes also known as St. Anthony of the Desert.
>
> To provide this unique chapel, two rooms have been thrown into one, the aisle is on one side, and the ten or twelve benches where the worshipers are seated are pushed close to the south wall. Probably 150 persons could be crowded into this little improvised chapel, which thus provides room for the Syrian colony of St. Louis, that all told does not much exceed that number.
>
> Those poor foreigners are mostly settled in the immediate neighborhood of their chapel. Most of them arrived in this city during the last few years; speaking the language of the country very imperfectly, they are greatly handicapped in their efforts to make a livelihood; the men work at whatever they can find to do, and the women keep house.

Serving this small congregation was the Reverend Father George Emmanuel, who came from the convent of San Roche, not far from Beirut, Lebanon. He arrived in St. Louis late in 1898, after a journey which first took him to Beirut, then Jerusalem, and from there to Alexandria. By steamer he proceeded to Marseilles, crossed France to Paris and Boulogne, thence by steamer to New York, then by train to St. Louis. Father Emmanuel served as the nucleus of the Lebanese colony in St. Louis, giving religious instruction to the children once a week in Arabic. There was no school attached to the chapel, so the children were educated at the cathedral school on Walnut Street.

Reverend Father George Emmanuel

In 1900 the Church of St. Anthony the Abbot was moved south and west to 717 South Third Street. Father Emmanuel's pastorate ended April 15, 1901. His replacement, Father Matthew Naimi, arrived October 17 of that year. In 1903 the church was moved to 615 South Broadway. A school was then established with two teachers and forty-five pupils. In August of that year, the first marriage in St. Louis according to the Maronite Rite was celebrated as a holiday event. Two years later Father Naimi left and was replaced by Father Anthony (Anton) Slyman.

In 1916 St. Anthony relocated at 1201 St. Ange Avenue. Father Anthony died October 15 of that year. Four priests followed him in quick succession--Fathers Mobarak Bellamah, George Assibelani, Gabriel Korgemos, and Francis Chamoun. The last of these was struck and killed by a streetcar. On February 4, 1921, Father Loakim Stephan, from Batroun by way of Johannesburg, South Africa, arrived. He served the church until its demolition in 1942 for a housing project. The church was never rebuilt.

By 1903 the local Lebanese population numbered six hundred and was settled from the river to Tenth Street and from Valentine to Gratiot. Their shops along Fourth Street and Broadway were crowded with goods such as St. Louis had never before seen--rare tobaccos, fancy embroidery, oriental carpets, brass of the finest workmanship. Their restaurants were duplicates of the coffee houses of the Near East. All about the area was different. It was a little bit of the Orient.

Their earliest local merchant appears to have been Neckley Ferris, who opened a dry goods shop in 1895 at 620 South Second Street. By the turn of the century, he had moved to the 600 block of South Fourth, rapidly becoming the business center of the Lebanese community. Other shops sharing that block during the first decade of the century were:

Assad George's Grocery, George Saffa's Grocery & Shoe Store, John G. Saffa's Dry Goods, Richard G. Saffa's Grocery. In the next block south were: Assad Saffar's Bakery (later to grow into the Columbia Ice Cream Cone Company and flourish until the late 1920's), Daniel Saffa's Dress Shop, and Richard G. Saffa's Confectionery. During the same period the 600 block of South Second Street also abounded with Lebanese shops. There Charles Abood and Nicholas Hydar pioneered with grocery stores.

However lively the area had appeared, it did not long remain the home of the Lebanese. Their community drifted southwest to the old northern edge of Frenchtown. This move began about 1915. There they established a business strip along Chouteau, converting old mansions to shops, with residences above. Included in the row were Namer Abood's Lace Shop, Joseph Aboussie's Grocery, Richard Aboussi's Restaurant, Samuel George's Confectionery, Wahby's Restaurant & Bar, Tony G. Azar's Dry Goods, Wani George's Family Ice Cream Cone Company--all lending a folksy air to the area. Hickory Street underwent a likewise transformation, though it did not become so heavily commercialized as did Chouteau. Families who had lived in the area for a half-century began to drift away. By the 1930's the area had become a Lebanese ghetto.

The heart of this community came to be the Church of St. Raymond. That maronite parish was organized July 15, 1913. The church, loyal to the papacy, but different in that the service is conducted in the ancient language of Aramaic, was served for its first thirty-two years by Father Joseph Karam, formerly assistant at St. Anthony the Abbot. He died in 1944, and the parish, unable to locate a replacement, was served by Father Stephan, formerly of St. Anthony the Abbot. He refused to accept the pastorate but was the nominal

(*Above*) Old Church of St. Raymond.
(*Below*) St. Raymond's Maronite Church.

priest until his death November 7, 1959. Attendance at the church dropped, and many members of the parish were absorbed into new neighborhoods in the suburbs. By the 1960's the Lebanese area south of Chouteau and east of Twelfth Street was rapidly being abandoned. Near the end of the decade, only ten families remained of what had once been a large neighborhood. No more than fifty families maintained ties with the Church of St. Raymond. It seemed as if the Lebanese community of St. Louis was about to vanish, but then came the renaissance.

In 1967 the Reverend Robert Shaheen arrived to serve the parish--the first leader of that flock since the death of Father Karam. Shaheen came to a scattered group and inherited a crumbling church building. Actually, the structure was an old limestone-faced double dwelling of the Second Empire style--long since drastically remodeled. An active campaign was begun to rebuild. The decision was made to keep the church at its old location. A new building was erected to its rear and was dedicated in the fall of 1975. A magnificent domed structure featuring small private courts, it stands as a proud complement to the beautiful office tower of Ralston Purina across Chouteau. Today the church is in the best of health and is crowded every time the doors are opened. Wednesdays and Thursdays the parish plays host to a businessman's luncheon, served in the nearby social hall. People of all ethnic groups come to partake of kibbi and other Lebanese favorites.

Several modern Lebanese businessmen have become celebrated in St. Louis. Steve Mizerany of the madcap television commercials offers his "square Deal" down on the Gravois. Eugene Slay, the trucking magnate, is a considerable power in Democratic politics. The Slay restaurants are likewise well-known. These men are worthy successors to their shopkeeper ancestors. However,

those Lebanese who have truly become superstars in the St. Louis firmament are those who went into politics.

The Seventh Ward, centering on the Lebanese neighborhood, produced Sorkis J. Webbe, once thought to be on his way to the office of Mayor. Paul Simon, President of the St. Louis Board of Aldermen, grew up on Hickory Street. And, that most remarkable of all St. Louis politicians, Ray Liesure, for thirty-one years Alderman of the Seventh Ward, was for many years the most talked-about of those children of the Levant. He was a politician of the old school. Hat on head and cigar in mouth, he was ever approachable by his constituents and sought to serve their needs. He died May 30, 1980. Those who had had their rounds with him were among the first to acknowledge the city's great loss. Recently a small park at Tucker Boulevard and Park Avenue was dedicated to his memory.

Today, the Lebanese of St. Louis are again a strong ethnic group. Their homes are scattered throughout the metropolitan area, but their hearts remain at St. Raymond's. LaSalle Street, rechristened as Lebanon Drive, shows the city's appreciation for the many contributions of this small but most vital nationality.

The Croatians

The least visible and smallest of the ethnic neighborhoods to develop in Frenchtown was that of the Croatians. Natives of what had been part of the Roman Province of Illyricum, and since tossed from one conqueror to another until the founding of the modern state of Yugoslavia, these people began settling in St. Louis as early as 1880. Their first neighborhood was near Arsenal and Broadway.

St. Joseph's Church. Twelfth and Russell.

Soulard Market years after the 1896 tornado destroyed the building.

In 1902 a gathering was held, and the St. Joseph Roman Catholic Church Society was organized. That same year the group purchased an old synagogue at Eleventh and Chouteau and rededicated the structure as St. Joseph's. Eight years later a parochial school was opened at 915 LaSalle.

Finding themselves in a neighborhood shifting rapidly to business and incoming Lebanese, the Croatians sought refuge further south into Frenchtown. In 1925 they bought the old Ursuline Convent at Twelfth and Russell. Two years later they built a new St. Joseph's at the site.

Through the years the Croatian community has clung together, and their church did not fall victim to the decline and lean years experienced by those of their neighbors, the Czechs and Lebanese. The Croatian singing and dancing societies are famous throughout the metropolitan area. There is a joyous spirit exhibited at Croatian gatherings such is rarely seen elsewhere in the area. No one had to remind the Croatians to search for their roots, as

they had never lost touch with them. Reflecting that ongoing pride is a bumper sticker which says, "Thank God I'm a Croatian."

These ethnic groups, the Czechs, Lebanese, and Croatians, saw Frenchtown through World War I, the great depression, and World War II. They heard Billy Sunday say, "Put it on the plate for Jesus." They laughed with the rest of America when Mae West told the cub scout, "Come back and see me when you're twenty-one." They kept Soulard Market alive for decades--long before it became chic to drive in from the suburbs to buy salt pork and turnips with the proletariat. But, after a half-century, even they have in large part left for other areas, proving once again that the only thing constant in Frenchtown is change itself.

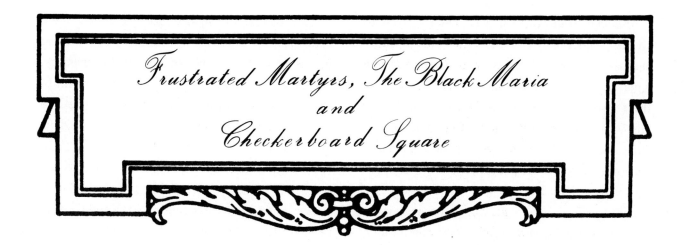

Frustrated Martyrs, The Black Maria and Checkerboard Square

It's not safe to walk out the door, day or night! Everywhere you turn there are muggings, rapes, and crimes of the vilest sort! What is the world coming to? Those were the thoughts of St. Louisans of the mid-nineteenth century, and they remain the thoughts of many St. Louisans after the passage of more than a century. In spite of man's efforts, poverty, crime, and ignorance survive.

St. Louis produced many who joined in the struggle to improve the lot of the lower classes. John Mullanphy started the local crusade, and in this century such as Father Dismas Clark ("The Hoodlum Priest"), Dr. Tom Dooley, and David P. Wohl continued to help the unfortunate. Frenchtown had its would-be saviors--dedicated, hardworking, and little-acclaimed. This is their story.

Although Frenchtown had its elegant avenues and mansions, they were but a facade, hiding alleys and narrow streets teeming with poorly-paid and ignorant working-class families. In the early years these were German peasants. In later years other immigrants jostled with these Germans to gain living space. In 1915 some areas in the community housed as many as 340 people to an acre. Squalor, such as many associate only with the back streets of Calcutta or East St. Louis, abounded near those elegant households of St. Louis' Near South Side.

Most sought to ignore the plight of these unfortunate people. One who did not do so was the Reverend W. E. Greene, an Episcopal missionary. Greene arrived in St. Louis in 1886 and was sent to Frenchtown to spread the Episcopal doctrine among the poor. On November 25, 1886, he held his first service upstairs over a grocery store at Third and Rutgers. Shortly afterward he moved to the southwest corner of Broadway and Park. For a season he held sway in a tent at Sixth and Gratiot. Greene's brave little group then found a home on

St. Stephen's Mission at Sixth and Rutgers.

Seventh Street just south of Hickory. They would remain there for eight years.

Episcopalians, working in an area peopled primarily by German Catholics--they invited ridicule. Garbage and dead animals were tossed into their quarters. They were called the vilest of names. It was not a job to be relished. One worker at the mission assessed the situation as follows:

> The neighborhood is made up of the lower and more ignorant class of German immigrants and their descendants, with all their reserve, pigheadedness and self satisfaction;--a more difficult combination of German stolidity and a cheap and false American independence: a little cleaner and a little better dressed than the Italian or Irish of the same class, but harder to approach and harder to move, wishing merely to be let alone in the enjoyment of their stupidity. This is the Germanic class that is not seeking education. It is a lower stratum and a stubbornly repulsing one, among whom it is necessary to instill the first spark of desire for something better. The appeal of educa-

Interior of St. Stephen's Mission.

tion was found futile and the book-learning side of St. Stephen's amounts now to practically nothing. The appeal of personal sympathy and friendship proved itself the only way.

Thus, both sides squared off to do battle. It was little wonder that the Episcopalians were slow to make inroads into the community.

In 1891 Gustavus Tuckerman came to head the small mission. His first job was to get the attention of the Germans. To do so, he organized a brass band and had it play in the street outside the mission's doors. The curious gathered, and Tuckerman invited them inside. There, he and his workers talked, but avoided preaching. People of the community found that they were free to come and go at will. Tuckerman felt that a positive atmosphere and a gradual elevation by association were the answers to luring his neighbors into the Episcopal fold. And so, the young mission began to attract a following. On Christmas Day, 1897, a new building was dedicated on the southeast corner of Sixth and Rutgers and christened as St. Stephen's

Kindergarten at St. Stephen's Mission. Lou Heger is fourth from left in second row.

Mission. Tuckerman had done an outstanding job. He left the work in 1901.

In 1901 the area surrounding St. Stephen's was the world to young Lou Heger. Born at 1226 South Seventh Street, he had lived all his life there. He attended kindergarten at St. Stephen's, and he played all day about the area streets. The sights, sounds, and smells, always changing, were a wonder to the child, and Lou never ceased to be fascinated.

By breakfast it had begun--masses of people were walking north up Seventh, and up Broadway, heading for work, window-shopping in the stores that stretched from Sidney Street to the French Market. In the evening those same masses would return, heading south, stopping briefly to purchase those items selected while passing in the morning. Lou left the house, temporarily joining the crowd, for his destination was the "convent lot," the former location of Sacred Heart Convent at the northwest corner of Broadway and Hickory. Usually there would be a ballgame organizing there, or better yet, a medicine show erecting its tent. If nothing was happening there, he might persuade his mother to part with a nickel--fare for the movie shown in the storefront on Broadway between Hickory and Rutgers--always a special treat. The discomfort of the hard straight chairs was immediately forgotten when the lights went out, the piano player began, and the screen (all of 10 x 15 feet) lit up with the customary slides, "Ladies Remove Hats," and "Gentlemen Don't Smoke." For the less than a hundred people packed into the small improvised theater, it was a marvel and a delight.

And then there were the temptations of Hahn's Ice Cream Parlor, just south of Rutgers on Broadway. On Saturday nights, after the neighbors had done their purchasing at the French Market, it was difficult to get into the place. It was always the French Market crowd at that hour, because Soulard didn't stay open in the evenings.

Sundays were always special. First came Sunday School at the First German Presbyterian Church up at the southwest corner of Tenth and Rutgers. There Reverend Jacob G. Kessler held sway, delivering sermons both in German and English. After church there was always the possibility of the family walking down to the river to board the steamboat "City of Providence" and going to Kimmswick for a picnic. And, of course, there was Eldracher's Saloon at Eighth and Hickory. Maybe his father would join the crowd flocking there to purchase "Dukeys," the small hamburgers that had made the place famous.

So the days went--all too rapidly. Everything came to a halt at 9 p.m. When the sound of the Liggett & Meyers whistle floated east to Frenchtown, every child headed for his stoop. Those few reluctant ones were always sought out by Dutch Fritz, the local policeman who could bounce a night club a block, projecting it precisely between a boy's legs. But, if all chores had been done perfectly, there might be one last joy of the day--to be allowed to go to the engine house at Broadway and Park to hear 9 o'clock strike. There a ritual was reenacted each evening. At the hour of nine, a bell would ring. The horses would dash forward to the doors, and the suspended harnesses would drop onto their backs to be secured by the firemen. It was a rare occasion when the harness hit the floor. If such occurred, the horses were backed up, and the drill began anew. And what it was like when it wasn't a drill! Then the black horses of the hose cart would come thundering down the street, "Hell to beat breakfast." At the same time the brown horses of the Salvage Corps, the "No. 2's," would come rushing from their house on Merchant Street, east of Broadway. It was always a race to see which team would first reach Seventh and Hickory. Once there was a tie and almost a disaster.

Yes, the area was never boring for an adventure-some child. Lou always hated to go to bed.

It was in 1901 that Henry Watson Mizner, a West Point graduate, took charge of St. Stephen's and "ruled the area with a rod of iron!" His wife, the foster-daughter of George A. Castleman, was a leader in St. Louis society. They were an odd pair in that neighborhood of small businesses and tenements, but they quickly gained the respect of all. They worked long hours and were always available to anyone who needed help--widows needing firewood, a youth seeking counseling, a drunken bum; all were welcomed and received help. They even brought a few laughs to the area. An annual minstrel show spotlighted local talent. A humorous parody of a newspaper, known as *Chewing Gum Squash*, reported bits of local gossip. The tone was light, the people chuckled, and Mizner

became a local hero. One article will suffice to show the affection which people in the area felt for the dedicated man.

EXTRA EXTRA EXTRA

"Episcopal Minister Chases Holy Roller Chicken" It was 9:25 a.m. on Sunday Morning Jan. 19, 1919 when much rumbling and shouting was heard in the rear of a residence at 602-4 Rutger St. Upon investigation it was perceived that a neighbor's chicken was causing much trouble by trying to make a get-a-way by way of a back yard. Much time and effort was exercised by Mrs. Berry and Louise who pursued the hunted chicken several times around the yard, until the chase-of-a-wild-goose came to a stand-still, the chicken having perched iself upon the fence. Fearing lest any movement made would send the chicken over the fence and

(*Opposite*) Firemen of Engine House 16.

(*Above*) Phoenix Fire Company # 7 was organized in the spring of 1843 to protect Frenchtown. Its motto was "Surgo Lucidus," and its president was Daniel H. Donovan. Located far to the south of other companies, the engine house was first in a frame building in the apex formed by the junction of Second, Broadway, and Park. In 1846, the brick building pictured was erected on the west side of Broadway, three doors north of Park. When called out by a fire alarm, the Phoenix Company drew its water from wells, ponds, and "sink-holes" long after the companies north of it were relying wholly on fire-plugs. The company colors were deep blue with silver mountings. Phoenix firemen appeared on parade with red merino shirts, trimmed with silver, white trousers, black leather belts, and blue, medium-crowned flat-topped hats. The volunteer company was disbanded and replaced with a paid company in November, 1857. The engine house then became # 16.

forever lost, the pursuers stood cornered trying to think of some new device or strategic movement they might make to get the all-important chick where it belonged whilst the neighbor woman remained at the opposite fence pleading that we please, oh please do this and that and the other thing. When to the Joy and Thankfulness of the pursuers, Mr. Mizner who happened to be passing down the street took the necessary steps to right the wrong by exclaiming in a quite natural tone of voice...Shoo-o-o which sent the chicken back in the yard, which was pursued by the yours-till-the-end and was caught in the corner and delivered to its owner, who we afterwards were informed was a Holy Roller, so that undoubtedly accounts for the Extraordinary Actions at the back yard fence. Although the trend of this little anecdote may not appeal very excitingly to its reader......allow me to assert that the affair in itself was a thriller. They say all Chicken Chasing is thrilling.

Mizner resigned and left St. Stephen's in April, 1926. He died four years later. By then, his work was known throughout the United States. Many compared his work to that of Jane Adams at Hull House in Chicago.

The work at St. Stephen's could not stop the decay of the surrounding area. By 1937 Sixth and Rutgers was the center of one of the worst slums in St. Louis. "Factories with soot and smoke...shut out fresh air and sun from the homes around." Crime was commonplace. On February 2, 1937, a customer in a bar at Broadway and Rutgers was taken to City Hospital for treatment of an injured hand. While there it was discovered that he was suffering from bullet wounds of both legs. He was unable to tell how he got the wounds. First he said he was shot by a woman. Then he said he was shot by a man, but was unable to tell where the shooting occurred.

The need for such an institution as St. Stephen's was greater than ever, but attendance at services was half what it had been in the 1920's. In 1948 word was circulating that a new highway was being projected through the area and might take the site of St. Stephen's. It was all so discouraging.

By 1952 the Third Street Expressway was under construction. Those early rumors proved to be so correct. The road went right over the site of the venerable mission. The decision was made to seek another location in the area, and thus, St. Stephen's Church was erected at Fourteenth and Park. There the poor are still served, no longer Germans, but the Negroes of the nearby housing projects. For almost a century St. Stephen's had been in the vanguard of social work in Frenchtown and will remain so as long as there is a need.

John G. Priest residence at Ninth and Chouteau, built in 1859 at a cost of $19,000 and maintained by sixteen slaves. U. S. Grant was a frequent visitor here.

154

On the northeast corner of Menard and Julia stands the once magnificent structure which housed the Presbyterian's answer to St. Stephen's. That Graeco-Roman ruin did service as the Menard Mission. Organized on July 10, 1875, the project functioned for two years at Eighth and Chouteau. In September, 1877, it was moved to quarters in the hall of Soulard Market and renamed as Soulard Market Mission. When the old market was destroyed by the tornado of 1896, the now-standing structure was begun. It was dedicated May 2, 1897. In assessing the value of this mission, one nineteenth-century Police Chief said, "The restraining influence of Soulard Market Mission is worth one hundred policemen a year to that part of the city." Time passed, and the empty and abandoned building is mute testimony that the conditions of the twentieth century eventually bested even those stubborn Presbyterians.

In the late 1940's the slums which had once been confined to the area near South Broadway began to expand. The western edge of Frenchtown, that region along South Thirteenth and Fourteenth streets, began to decline rapidly. In 1955 the entire area was demolished to make way for the construction of Darst-Webbe Housing Project. Preservationists shuddered as they saw block-after-block of once elegant houses being swept away. In the 1100 block of South Thirteenth stood that mammoth twenty-five-unit row of townhouses known as Larned Row. Constructed in 1859 at a cost of $75,000, the group had once represented the last word in luxury housing. Now they were being replaced by government-subsidized housing.

Menard Mission. Now being rehabilitated.

Larned Row. Longest row of townhouses ever built in St. Louis.

Everyone hoped that the new high-rise blocks of apartments would be the city's answer to replacing substandard dwellings. They proved to be a sorry answer, and hope died quickly. Elevators and landings became the lurking places for thugs, rapists, and a motley assortment of the perverse and profane. Those who could fled the project, leaving behind the old and feeble and young mothers nursing large families. In a short time the mammoth buildings had become more notorious than any slum since the old days of Clabber Alley and Castle Thunder!

That northern part of Frenchtown not demolished for highway construction and housing projects became an isolated island. Business continued to encroach, vacancy rates soared, and crime came to be a way of life. The Lebanese, the last to hold out in the area, began to flee to safer and more hospitable parts of the metropolitan area. Even the neighborhoods south of the highway and beyond Soulard Market were affected by the social and economic decline. Just how badly so was revealed by the tragic event which occurred New Years Day, 1961--the murder of Barbara Jean Black.

Ninth and Russell had once been the site of the elegant Russell mansion and later Union Park. But by 1961 the name "Union Hill" designated only a particular part of a sordid bunch of rundown houses. The area where once crowds had danced and made merry in a pleasant beer garden now became the scene for murder. The killing, still unsolved, was that of a thirteen-year-old girl.

156

Beaten and strangled, her body was found in an alley behind 1003 Russell. The child had met her assassin while returning home from a double feature at the Apachee Theater. St. Louis was stunned.

The murder focused the city's attention on the decaying area. What was revealed was shocking. The *Post-Dispatch* reported:

> It was a white area in which every other household seemed to harbor a member who had seen the inside of the Biggs Building for the Criminally Insane at Fulton State Hospital or the Missouri State Penitentiary at Jefferson City or the Workhouse or the City Jail. It was a neighborhood that had its winos and its drunks, its spats and its jealousies--which led interviewing officers to comment in their reports that "the whole family is nuts" and "This guy is as loose as a box of corn flakes."

One person interviewed said she had heard a girl scream, "Please, don't do that to me," and another voice say, "Get her into the car." The girl who overheard did not interrupt her television viewing, because she said that sort of thing happened every day in her neighborhood. The bizarre setting, as threatening and as frightening as any scene from Caligari's Cabinet, gripped the city's attention, and all eyes gazed with morbid fascination on old Frenchtown.

Most of those viewing the situation considered it to be hopeless, but even then, when the area was wallowing in such filth and squalor, dreamers were planning to resurrect the area and build it anew. The Apachee Theater and its dingy neighbors would soon fall before the wrecking ball. South Broadway and Seventh Street would be rebuilt as modern shopping and office areas. And, in that region which had once seemed like a little bit of Bohemia and Lebanon, plans were being prepared for that most ambitious of projects, LaSalle Park.

LaSalle Park

William H. Danforth's death on Christmas Eve, 1955, ended one of the most remarkable careers in St. Louis business history. He had founded and presided over a company that had become a corporate giant, with plants and outlets around the globe. He remained Chairman of the Board to the end. He kept his headquarters in Frenchtown and his feet on the ground.

Many considered Mr. Danforth's folksy manner to border almost on eccentricity. Every day he took a mile walk at noon, striking up conversations with whomever he met along the way, listening more often than talking. He was ever receptive to new ideas and always alert to change and possibilities. He authored several works, his most popular book being *I Dare You*, an excellent delineation of his philosophy--one stressing a positive approach to life and a belief that anything is possible if approached in the proper manner. Danforth's own life and career were an excellent vindication of that philosophy. He represented the American Dream-- honest young man who works hard, lives a clean life, and becomes a very rich man. *Luck and Pluck, Strive and Succeed*, or any of those other Horatio Alger titles would have suited a biography of the man.

Danforth graduated from Washington University in 1892. He then went to work in the brick business, but quickly saw that the demand was seasonal. He knew good advice when he heard it; "Animals must eat the year round." Joining in partnership with George Robinson and William Andrews, he

William H. Danforth

chartered the Robinson-Danforth Commission Company on January 8, 1894, dealing in horse and mule feed. Danforth noted that the traditional feeds were rather limited--oats, corn, and hay. Oats were expensive, and corn often caused colic. Danforth began experimenting with new mixtures and processes. Innovation was to become his constant preoccupation.

The young firm suffered a disastrous setback when the tornado of 1896 demolished its mill at Twelfth and Gratiot. Danforth went to a bank and secured a loan, using his baby as collateral. A new mill went up at Eighth and Gratiot. About 1898 history was made. The firm began production of a whole-wheat breakfast food called Purina Wheat. The name had been coined to signify purity. The product quickly became popular, and many people began to refer to the firm as Purina Mills, still a common nickname.

At the turn of the century, the Ralston Health Club had a nation-wide membership of 800,000. Dr. Ralston's book, *Life Building*, recommended a whole-wheat cereal. Danforth contacted him and worked out a deal. Dr. Ralston tested Purina Wheat and reported that it "had no superior." The product's name was changed to Ralston Health Food, and the good doctor recommended it to his followers. By 1902 the Ralston and Purina names were so famous that Danforth's business was renamed as Ralston Purina Company. The distinctive checkerboard logo was also adopted at that time.

When the Louisiana Purchase Exposition opened in St. Louis, Ralston Purina was ready. Samples of their various products were given to the hundreds of thousands of visitors to the city. These visitors carried away their gifts, and the word was spread

to the world of the excellence of Danforth's products. It also helped that those products (cereal foods, flour, and feeds) had all won first prizes at the Fair. It was a grand bit of promotion, but typical of Danforth's gift for taking advantage of opportunity.

During the next five decades Danforth saw his company expand dramatically. Over sixty manufacturing plants dotted the globe. Ralston Purina became the world's largest producer of balanced rations for livestock and poultry, and a major manufacturer of breakfast foods. The company's headquarters, Checkerboard Square, came to be one of the most famous addresses in history, and it remained located where it had always been, at the northern edge of old Frenchtown.

In the 1950's and early 1960's, many downtown firms moved their offices to beautiful campus locations in St. Louis County. There was pressure for Ralston Purina to follow suit. However, Danfort's spirit must have been surveying the scene and communicating the message, "I Dare You." The decision was made to stay put and build at the old site. It was a brave decision, because the surrounding area was anything but inviting.

By the mid-1960's the residential area south of Ralston Purina was in a desperate condition-- peopled in large part by poor whites who had fled the cotton fields of Southeast Missouri and Arkansas, filled with old deteriorating housing (out of 875 dwelling units east of Twelfth Street, 800 were regarded as substandard), and crime rampant. No one was happy with the situation, least of all the people who lived there. Something had to be done.

In 1965 the Ten-Park Neighborhood Improvement Association was formed. The 150 households comprising the group felt that they could save the neighborhood. They organized an operation boot-strap and raised $1,000. This was the fund with which a large rundown neighborhood was to be restored! City Hall sounded out the people in the

Ralston Purina Tower

area concerning the possibility of urban renewal. It was found that few in the area favored such a scheme. However, few in the area favored any scheme, as a survey indicated that 63% of the inhabitants were only interested in leaving.

Alfonso J. Cervantes, then Mayor of St. Louis, approached the officials of Ralston Purina and asked if they would participate in a renewal effort for the area. Ralston agreed. Neighborhood meetings were again held. Promises were made that any renewal program would be different from those of the past. People would be paid the fair market value for their property, relocation settlements would be made, and present residents would be given first priority in attaining new housing in the area. Hearing this, the members of Ten-Park agreed to support such a renewal effort.

LaSalle Park Redevelopment Corporation, named for two streets in the area, was set up. The boundaries established were Gratiot, Seventh, Twelfth, and the Third Street Expressway. Ralston Purina agreed to donate up to $2,000,000 to match federal funding. From the beginning this program was different. Never before had a renewal effort been undertaken in an area peopled by whites. Never before had there been a program involving federal, state, and local government programs, as well as a major commercial firm. Never before had a program been destined to be so plagued by delays and changes of plans.

In March, 1969, the 137 acres comprising the project were declared blighted. St. Louis Land Clearance for Redevelopment Authority then applied for a federal planning grant. The government scrapped the plan. In 1970 the local agency again applied. The new office in Washington, HUD, approved $4,000,000 for the program, and shortly afterward invalidated the grant, saying it had made a "mistake." In February, 1971, HUD reversed its earlier decision and again approved

federal funds for LaSalle Park. However, money did not arrive in St. Louis until January, 1972. Land Clearance then began acquiring property and relocating families. The first demolition in the area occurred in December, 1972, when several old houses at Ninth and LaSalle were razed. On the scene were Mayor Cervantes, R. Hal Dean (Chairman of the Board of Ralston Purina) and Representative Leonor K. Sullivan. During the following year about seventy houses were leveled in the area between LaSalle and Hickory. An impressive open space was created, and it remained open, because the Nixon Administration chose that time to freeze federal housing funds.

LaSalle Park had been designed to be a mixture of residential, commercial, and light industrial properties. Ninth Street was to run directly south from Chouteau to Park. All the lands east of that street were designated to be developed for light industry. The residential properties would be west of Ninth Street. New townhouses would be placed among rehabilitated older houses. This plan didn't exactly work out.

Preservationists objected that not enough of the old houses were being saved. Residents objected that nothing was being done. The latter fled. The former wept as empty buildings were vandalized and quickly succumbed to the elements. Some inhabited structures were in such bad condition that they did not survive the delays. A little old lady was startled by a noise at the rear of her house at 1302 South Tenth Street. When she went to investigate, she found that the back of her house had fallen off. A few stoic souls took it all in stride. A woman on Morrison Street remarked, "Aw, hell. It's not so bad anymore. All the people I never liked have left. At last I've gotten rid of my neighbors."

In February, 1974, the go-ahead was given by Washington to begin the construction of 148 low-income apartments. One frustrated journalist who had followed the situation over the years philosophically noted, "A thirsty Irishman would have brought his paycheck home to his wife in less time." By the summer of 1975, a few units were available to renters. The following year they were completed and filled. Few of the original inhabitants of the area chose to live in them. They took their money and left. For a considerable time this apartment complex would stand alone in the redevelopment area. LaSalle Park was again stalled, and plans were being redrawn.

In 1975 a most fortunate change was made in the concept of LaSalle Park. Those buildings still standing and of architectural merit would be saved and restored. New streets would be built, brick sidewalks put down, period lighting installed, and

extensive landscaping undertaken. Plans were completed and sufficient red tape cut so that Ralston Purina and the Redevelopment Authority could begin marketing the properties late in 1976.

The news caught the imaginations of St. Louisans. Prospective buyers flocked to the area. What had seemed to be a hopelessly-stalled project had suddenly become the most exciting development in St. Louis neighborhood restoration. New homeowners signed agreements binding them to a set of guidelines which restricted choices of exterior materials and colors. Such crude methods as sandblasting and exterior metal trims were prohibited. Interiors could be handled in any manner suitable to the buyer, just so long as the house complied with the city code eighteen months

Isaiah Sellers residence. Captain Sellers was the most famous boatman ever to navigate the Mississippi. He was the "original" Mark Twain. He built his house on the northwest corner of Ninth and Hickory in 1850. It was demolished in the 1960's.

after the date of purchase.

Ralston Purina completely rehabilitated a row of 1860 townhouses at Tenth and Morrison. Around the corner they restored the exteriors of another row. The Redevelopment Authority did extensive work to a scattered group of structures. With the evidence of such major commitments by these two groups, individuals purchased the remaining buildings, and work was begun throughout the area. By 1980 LaSalle Park was well on its way to becoming an elegant neighborhood once more. Beautiful residential rows now stand where just a few years before had only been dilapidated, abandoned, and gutted structures.

This project proved most successful as regards commercial development. Lohr Distributing, A.D.T. Security, Security Armored Car, Winney Printing Co., Kinder Care, and others, soon transformed vacant blocks into one of the most attractive industrial areas of the city. LaSalle Park finally succeeded! Setbacks had proved to be just that, only setbacks!

Many people deserve credit for the reclamation of such a large area. Many at Ralston Purina labored for years to bring this dream to fulfillment. But, probably none other spent as much time, suffered through so many hectic hours seeking solutions to problems, and received less reward for their time than did Fred Perabo and John D. Fox, who headed up the project. Always supporting them were R. Hal Dean and John Baird. These leaders of Ralston Purina gave the project top management approval. Standing at their side and always offering assistance were James M.

1300 block of South Tenth. Built c. 1860.

Antebellum house with mansard roof later added.

Murray and Vern Thurmer of St. Louis Land Clearance and Redevelopment. These men, like Greene, Tuckerman, Mizner, and others before them, rendered a service for Frenchtown of monumental proportion.

Today LaSalle Park stands as a model of urban redevelopment. It isn't finished yet, but such efforts take time, and probably for the best. The delays which the project encountered ultimately resulted in a better-planned and balanced result.

Former residents drive through the area and are proud to say they once lived there. Others pour through the streets on weekends and marvel at what has been accomplished in such a short time. And, people walk the streets again where just a few years before no one either cared or dared to do so.

Through the Looking Glass

For years I wandered the streets of St. Louis marvelling at the beautiful and quaint architecture that survived from the nineteenth century. And, for years, I dreamed of moving into house after house, only to wait and see each fall victim to the wrecking ball. I joined the crowds flocking to Lafayette Square's yearly house tours. I trecked through Campbell House and through the DeMenil Mansion. I dreamed, but I never seriously considered moving into the city. Secretly I thought, "God, people are crazy who attempt to restore old houses!" And then I found LaSalle Park.

I was a typical county resident, living in a condominium in South County, making occasional forays into downtown to shop. Each time I drove down Highway 55, I noticed the beautiful St. Vincent de Paul complex and a particularly ugly and charming dwelling across the street, 911 Park. The house was a beacon calling to me, but I was slow to respond. After years of noticing it, one day I decided the time had come for closer inspection. I got off the highway, drove around to the site, and fell in love with what was to become LaSalle Park.

I was amazed by the area's architecture and by its neglect. When I stopped by the church, the priest informed me that the neighborhood was scheduled for demolition. I thought, "Oh well, why get excited! So you like the neighborhood. It's abandoned, rundown, and scheduled to be demolished. Take a few pictures, like you've always done, and forget it."

But I couldn't forget it. Time after time I kept driving back into the neighborhood. I took pictures and I walked around. The more I did so, the more I knew that there was something special about this place. This was where I wanted to be.

And then one day came the great news. On one of my periodic ventures into the area, I saw windows and doors being boarded up and a fence being erected around the area. This didn't look like the first step to demolition. An inquiry at the office of Landmarks left me ecstatic: the area was to be restored! Ralston Purina had had a change of heart and had decided to save those structures which remained. A concerted effort was going to be made to bring the area back to some semblance of its former glory!

I immediately made an appointment to see 911 Park--my first love. After years I would be going into the house I had thought so much about, and I would be there as a prospective buyer!

After going through the house, I asked to see

what else was available, convinced that I would be back to claim 911 Park. However, when I entered what I had considered to be my second choice, 916 Hickory, I knew that was the house for me. In five minutes I asked to purchase the house. I went home with the assurance that no one except myself would be considered as a possible buyer. I got on the phone and called everyone to tell them I had bought a house. Most responded with, "Have you been drinking again?"

Red tape and years of confused bureaucratic material had to be poured through before the sale was final. After five months of deliberation, the attorneys for Ralston and Land Clearance, the developers, felt they were ready to conclude the sale. On March 9, 1977, I presented my check and left with the deed to my house. I was the first new homeowner in LaSalle Park!

Renovation was begun almost immediately. Soon workmen were swarming over the old house. Plaster came tumbling down, shingles were cast to the wind, trash came up from the basement, and flimsy partitions were removed. When the third-floor walls were taken down, an interesting discovery was made--they had been constructed from thousands of old Chinese checker boards!

The house was in surprisingly good condition and retained almost all its original appointments: marble mantles (though painted many times), a beautiful walnut staircase (also painted numerous times), and a fantastic chimney in the kitchen, complete with a walk-in fireplace. In a whirlwind of work, the house was made habitable again. Supposedly the work was to be completed by June 15. Naive in such affairs, I accepted the contractor's word that the house would be ready. I sold my condominium and made arrangements to move June 23rd, and did so.

What a mess! I moved into a house without windows, no electricity, no phone, and running water only in a third-floor bathroom. Weeks later I was still trying to create some semblance of order. How do you cope with a phone company that insists your residence is a vacant lot--especially after they had prewired the house weeks before! There must be someone who will appreciate the irony in having the only house for blocks with new wiring and that being the only house without electric service (the electric company was just a bit slow in coming to hook up the house!) In the meantime, sixty empty houses surrounding mine still had electric service! My problem was temporarily solved by climbing into the third-story window of the house next door and running an extension cord into my house, so that I could use small appliances. Then I learned that I could get no garbage pickup or mail delivery. It seems that these two agencies were foiled by the fence surrounding the neighborhood. Such minor inconveniences were the story of my first summer and winter in LaSalle Park.

Little other work was done in the area that first year. Life was quiet, if a bit isolated, and work continued on my still-incompleted house. By the next spring, some nine months after I had moved in, the painters departed, the yard was cleaned and readied for planting, the fence around the neighborhood came down, new streets were built, and work began on surrounding houses. LaSalle Park was finally on the move!

I now felt like an old hand, and it was interesting to take note of the new arrivals to the neighborhood. One neighbor, as new to the job of rehabilitation as I had been, pulled up in her sports car, got out in her designer jeans, and entered her house with one cloth and a can of cleanser intent upon cleaning her house before the workmen arrived. Some minutes later, after getting myself under control, I went over, introduced myself, and explained the futility of such action at that stage of the job. She thanked me, saying "What would I ever do without you," and left.

With a smattering of neighbors moving in during the summer and fall of 1978, the area was no longer so forbidding in appearance. A few flowers bloomed, bright curtains went up, and the tourists arrived. "Do you live here?" became a frequent query, followed by "You know, I was born here. Could we go through the house?" The first few times I heard those lines, I fell for them. But after awhile the number of repeaters was such that my house would have had to have been a foundling institution to have accommodated so many youngsters!

And then came the creation of the neighborhood organization--the LaSalle Park Homeowners Association. I was asked to run for president and to share my experiences with the group. At the time I decided to decline and keep my mouth shut, so as not to discourage those new to the game. The meetings soon demonstrated the need for such a

sounding board. Complaints were often petty, but they were genuine to those voicing them. Homeowners got to know each other and soon anticipated what each would say. It could be said that LaSalle Park had reached maturity. We now had our own gossip, our own trouble makers, and our own eccentrics--what more did we need? A history of the area, of course!

As an historian I had often mused about the area's past. However, a year elapsed after I moved in before I had time to start researching the area. Of course, I began with my house. I wanted to know when it was built and by whom. After months of research, I had compiled an exhaustive dossier on the family--the Olshausens, German newspaper magnates of the nineteenth century. While attending a small party in Webster Groves, the hostess, knowing my love for research, asked what project I had recently been working on. I replied, "The Olshausen Family." A friend present said,

Gustavus Mueller and John Pullis mansions in foreground.

168

Tenth and Morrison. A Pullis ironfront.

937 Morrison Avenue

"Why, I think that is one of my families." It proved to be. I went out to Ladue to interview other descendants. Out came their old photograph albums. There were all sorts of 1880's photographs of the area now known as LaSalle Park. Also included was a sheet of housenumbers of the various residences, of which mine was one.

I looked at the numbers in shock! They were not the same as the numbers I had been working with! I had known that the house numbers were no longer the same as they had originally been, but I had not known that the numbers had been changed more than once! It was quickly apparent that I had researched not my house, but my side yard! I had to start all over. And I had been so proud of the Olshausens!

I returned to the libraries and soon was tracing the true builders of my house, who proved to be just as fascinating as the family I had first researched. Then, I decided I may as well check out the house on the other side of mine. I kept on right down the block, only to find that I had stumbled into a fascinating nineteenth-century neighborhood. It was as if a time warp had occurred, and I had been transported back to the past century. What was at first a preoccupation soon became an addiction. I came to dwell in the libraries. I traced many of the families who had helped build the original neighborhood, and they generously shared their family documents and oral histories. The result is the preceding chapters of this work.

Some description ought now be given of that part of Frenchtown that survives as LaSalle Park.

900 block of Morrison Avenue.

171

It is unlikely that Ralston had in mind the saving of what was a distinct neighborhood subdivision from its beginnings, but that is just what has occurred. On June 22, 1857, at ten a.m., 250 lots were auctioned in D. D. Page's Southern Addition. That property stretched from Hickory Street south to Park and from Eighth Street to Eleventh. Thus, what is now LaSalle Park's "historic area" is the old eastern end of D.D. Page's subdivision.

Few houses were erected right away, for 1857 was a year of economic depression in the United States. It appears that the first house built in Page's Southern Addition still stands at the southwest corner of Ninth and Rutgers streets. This was the residence of P. E. Burke, attorney, which was built in the summer of 1857. Burke, a native of Ireland, had lived in St. Louis from his infancy and was admitted to the bar in 1849. In 1854 he was elected to the legislature. When the Civil War approached, he joined the German home guards and was present at the capture of Camp Jackson. During the war he rose to the rank of Colonel. Burke died a hero's death. His body was returned to St. Louis, and a magnificent funeral was conducted for him from St. Vincent de Paul on June 6, 1864. Generals Rosecrans, Gray, and Trotter were in attendance. Military bands and infantry companies paraded in the streets with arms reversed. Mayor Thomas of St. Louis was a pallbearer.

In later years a three-story addition was added to

923 and 925 Rutgers Street.

the front of Burke's dwelling, and it was converted to a commercial building. The longest use for the structure was as Schobel's Ice Cream Parlor and Bakery. As such, it was the favorite hangout for children of the area in the early 1900's. In later years it became a hangout of a different sort as the 900 Bar. Today, the building is being restored to its former elegance.

Several structures were built in the area in 1859, but only one survives, the John Pullis residence at 916 Hickory. Built at a cost of $5,000, the house was one of the more sophisticated ones erected in Page's subdivision. The iron porch on the side, formerly gracing the front of the house, was among the first in St. Louis and is the last to survive. The window and door lintels of the house are iron. The iron all came from Pullis' own foundry. After the Pullis

family moved, the house was rented by Enno Sander. Sander was one of the most prominent of the German immigrants, having been Assistant Secretary of War in Baden, Germany, and owner of his own chemical factory in St. Louis. He was a founder of the St. Louis College of Pharmacy, and was for forty-six years Treasurer of the St. Louis Academy of Science. In later years the building served as a boarding house before being purchased by the Simon family. This Lebanese family held the house for over fifty years. After it was abandoned, neighborhood kids made it their playhouse.

The 1860's saw the virtual completion of the neighborhood. Few buildings were erected after that decade, except as infill in what were formerly yards, or as replacements for houses destroyed by fire. The most impressive of these structures now

Contemporary view of the library in the Pullis mansion.

Dining Room in the Pullis mansion as it now appears.

standing were both built in 1868, one on the northwest corner of Ninth and Morrison, and the other at 912 Hickory. The two houses today represent the extremes in the neighborhood's redevelopment.

The house on Morrison was built by Dr. Charles Ferdinand Hauck, physician and surgeon, and a native of Kur Hessen, Germany. Dr. Hauck used the east wing of the house as his medical office. The yard was devoted almost exclusively to a cactus garden. The Haucks lived in the residence until the early 1900's before moving to Flora Boulevard. In later years the structure served various purposes, among them being a home for wayward boys. Anyone coming into the neighborhood is struck by the building's architectural beauty and grandeur. However, little has yet been done toward its restoration, and the prospect is that its rehabilitation could be stalled by lengthy court maneuvers. It

(*Above*) Enno Sander.
(*Below*) Dr. Charles Hauck's residence and office at Ninth and Morrison.

(*Above*) Charlie Berger's rehabilitated apartment house on South Thirteenth Street. One of the many such structures in the Soulard area of Frenchtown. (*Opposite*) Interior of the above.

is sad to say that even in a neighborhood designed to keep out profiteers, the Hauck house appears to have fallen into the hands of an unscrupulous speculator. The house at 912 Hickory Street has fared much better.

Gustavus F. Mueller, partner in the wholesale grocery firm of Meyer & Meister, built with a taste and sense of elegance possessed by few of his neighbors. When he moved in 1880, William C. Popp, architect and builder, took up residence in the grand house. The Popps remained at that address until the early 1900's. 912 Hickory was substantially altered by disaster and by man. The 1896 tornado removed the attic level at the rear of the house, and it was never rebuilt. A store front was added and the front-parlor floor lowered to ground level. The total effect was most displeasing to the eye. Thieves removed the marble mantels,

the stair railing, and the storm doors. Luckily, the latter were returned. Also fortunate was the fact that someone with money, and an inclination to spend it, acquired the dwelling. Funds were lavished upon the structure. The result is most impressive, if not a little too much so. The only criticism that could be leveled is that the house is overrestored: the patina of age was buffed away, antique marble mantels now gleam as if new, and furnishings from Sotheby Park Bernet abound. All is near perfection, spit and polish, and the talk of St. Louis.

LaSalle Park has definitely arrived. The cocktail set is once again entrenched east of Tucker Boulevard. Allan Rocky Lane no longer rides at the White Wave, and the last customer long ago stepped out at Vince's Step In Bar. Only one Lebanese mother and her family remain in the area, and the Czechs have long vanished. But, a new neighborhood is building, and it promises to be a good one. Many of the settlers find the setting to be as different for them as it was to those immigrants of the past. But, like those who came before them, they are quickly adjusting to life in the very heart of the city, and now speak of the place as home. And, like those of the past had mused, "Who knows what the future holds in store for them?" I only hope it will be half as interesting as what has come before.

As the patient reader has observed, Frenchtown has passed through many stages in the last two centuries. A pastoral setting, dotted with a few elegant houses, gave way to what was the most exciting and varied neighborhood of nineteenth-century St. Louis. People of national importance called the area home. Businesses that grew to be world-famous had their birth and still flourish there. Immigrant groups came and departed; yet some still commute back to their churches on Sundays. Recent years have seen social experi-

ments, massive reclamation projects, and a recent emphasis on saving the old and blending it with the new. In effect, Frenchtown is St. Louis in microcosm.

Call the present area whatever you will--La Salle Park, Soulard, the Projects, the Near South Side--but never call it boring. It is true that some Philistines insist that they can't discern the charm which those present residents claim for the neighborhood. Frequently do the people of the area hear, "You're too close to the downtown. The houses are too big and drafty. Wouldn't you like to be closer to a country club and a Baskin-Robbins?" To answer such critics I would borrow from that noted sage, Dickson Terry. He spoke our feelings when he remarked, "We love you for the very things that fools despise you for."

A Unique View Of Frenchtown

In 1875 a monumental work was undertaken by Camille N. Dry. He drew the entire city of St. Louis, presenting it as if seen from the air and from the southeast. The resulting book, *Pictorial St. Louis, The Great Metropolis of the Mississippi Valley*, designed and edited by Rich. J. Compton, was copyrighted the following year. It is a beautiful work and is a rare depiction of a nineteenth-century city.

Every building, tree, haystack, outhouse, and wayfaring stranger was captured in this huge volume. There are some mistakes (occasionally a building is shown reversed), and some buildings are shown as completed, when in fact they were not so for a number of years (Sts. Peter and Paul Church, for instance). Interspersed between the pages of drawings are histories of many of the businesses and public institutions of St. Louis. The book is thus of immense value to researchers and lovers of St. Louis history.

In 1979 Riverside Press reprinted Compton and Dry's great work. Thus, for the first time in this century, the book was made readily available to the public. Few had known it, because it previously could be found only in rare book collections. The writer often used this work as a guide in researching *Frenchtown*. Those pages which follow are taken directly from Camille N. Dry's collection of drawings. They truly present a unique view of Frenchtown.

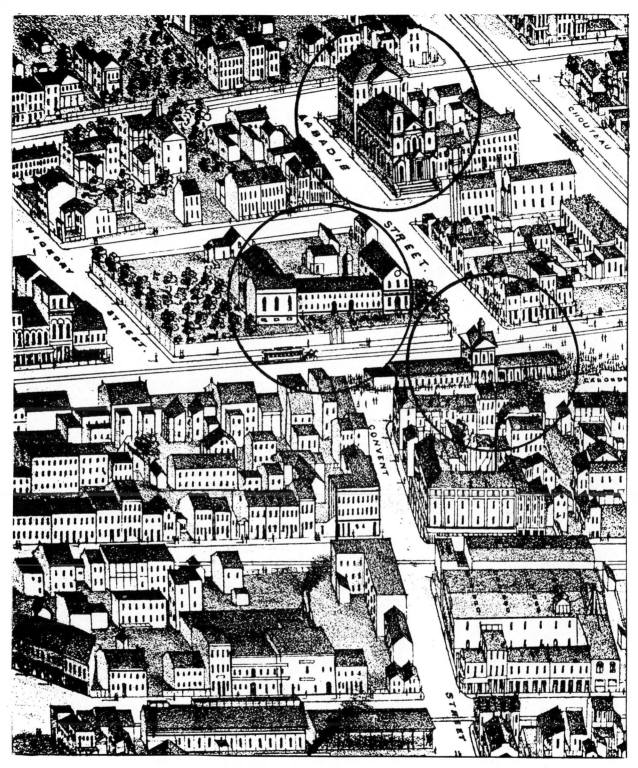

(*Top Circle*) Annunciation Church.

(*Lower Left Circle*)   Convent of the Sacred Heart.

(*Lower Right Circle*) French Market.

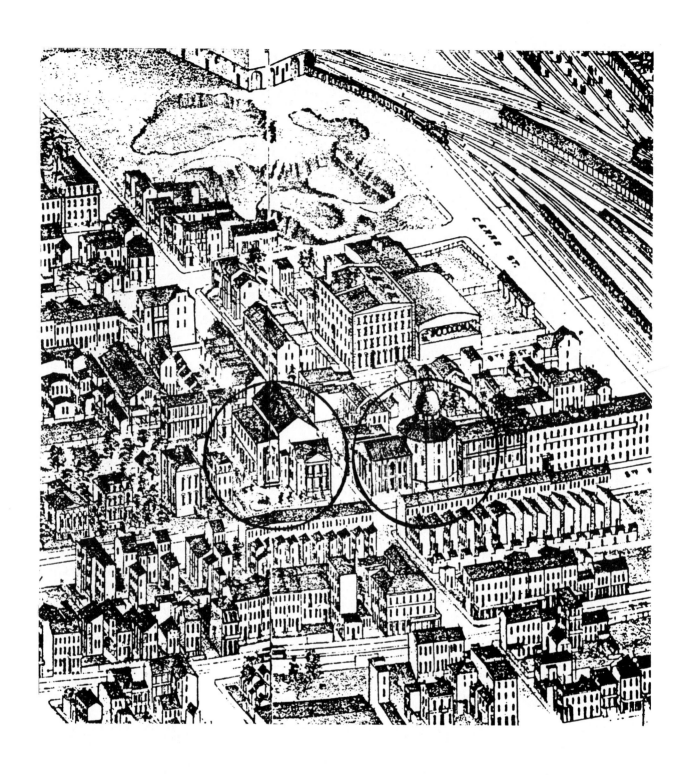

(*Left Circle*) Germania Club (old James Harrison mansion).
(*Right Circle*) McDowell's Medical School. Gratiot Street Prison during the Civil War.

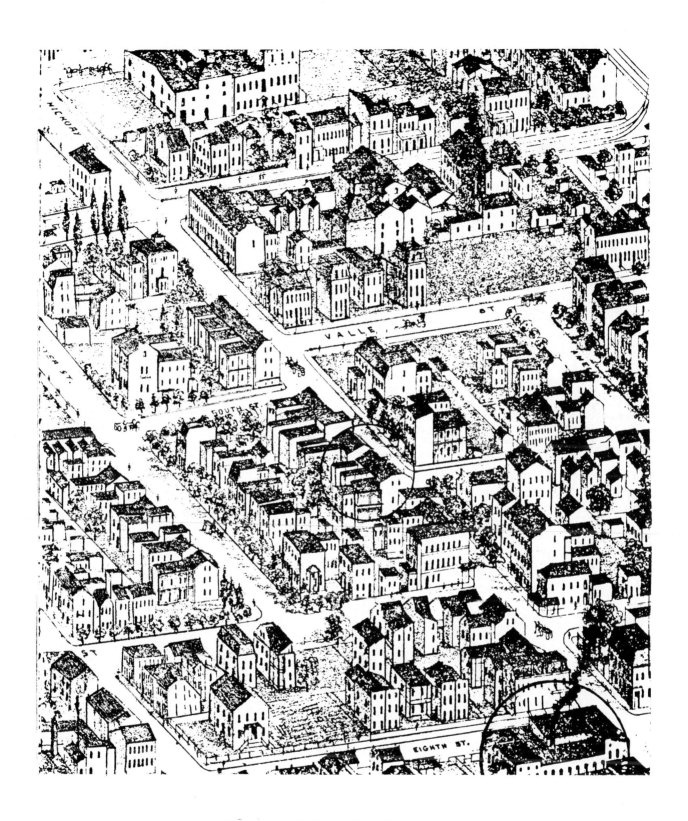

(*Top circle*) Pullis and Mueller mansions.
(*Bottom circle*) Pullis Ironworks.

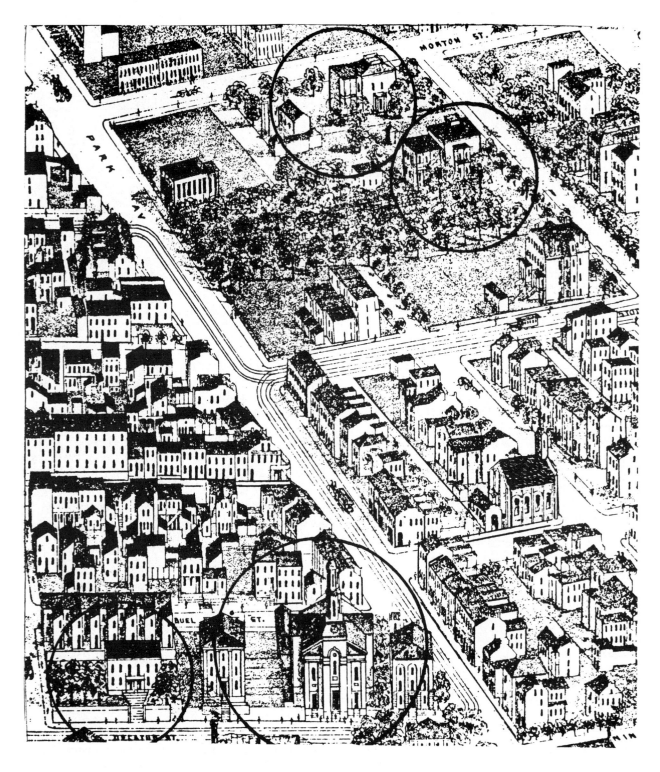

(*Top Circle*) Henry D. Bacon mansion. Next to it in circle is the Daniel D. Page residence.

(*Lower Left Circle*) Julia Soulard mansion. Circle to right of it encloses St. Vincent de Paul Church.

(*Top Circle*) Pullis Ironworks.

(*Bottom Circle*) Pelagie Rutgers mansion.

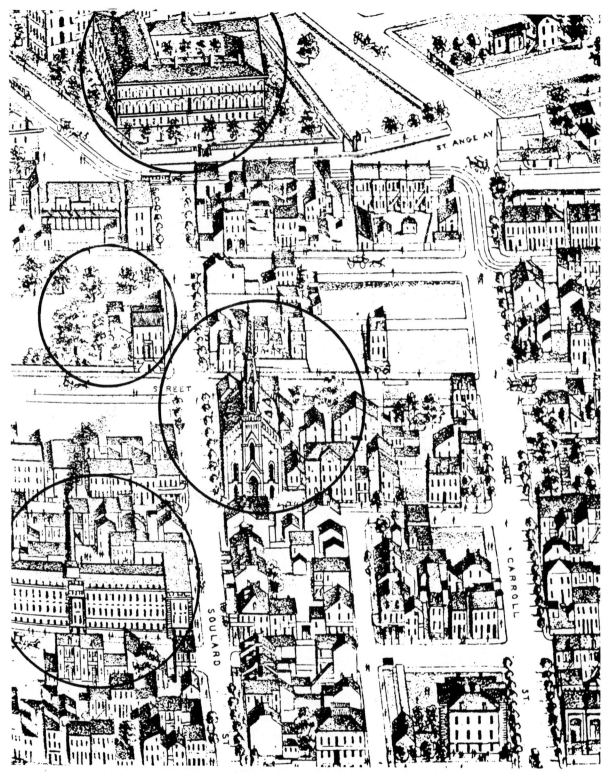

(*Top Circle*) City Hospital. Circle below it contains the Henry G. Soulard mansion. The next circle down encloses St. John Nepomuk Church.

(*Bottom Circle*) Meier Cotton Factory.

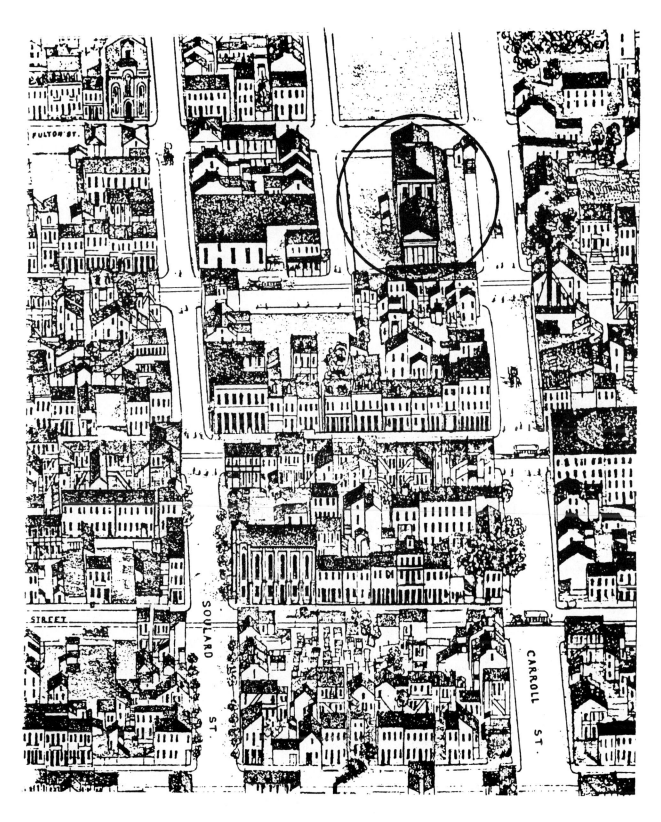

(*Circle*) Soulard Market.

(*Circle*) William Russell mansion.

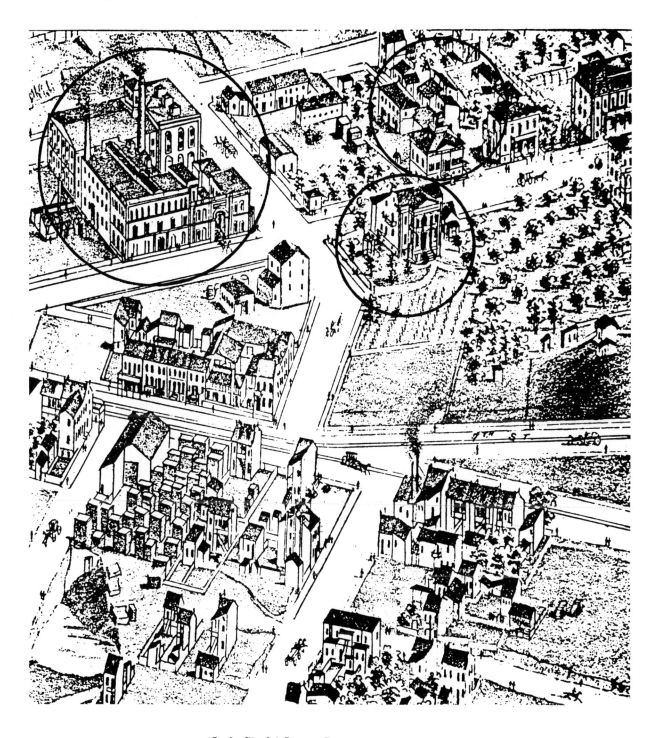

(*Left Circle*) Lemp Brewery.

(*Top Right Circle*) Adam Lemp mansion.

(*Bottom Circle*) DeMenil mansion.

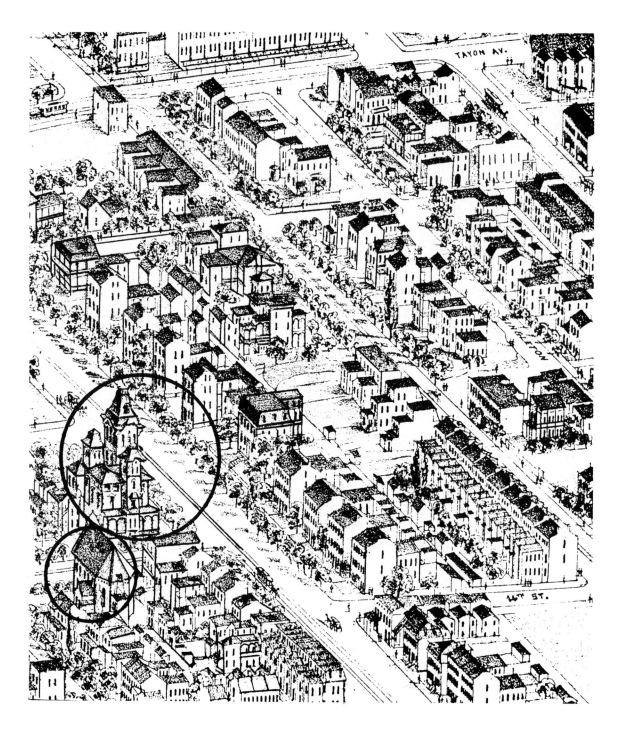

(*Top Circle*) Cracker Castle, once St. Louis' most talked-about house. Located at Fourteenth and Chouteau.

(*Bottom Circle*) Church of the Holy Angels.

(*Circle*) Sts. Peter and Paul Church.

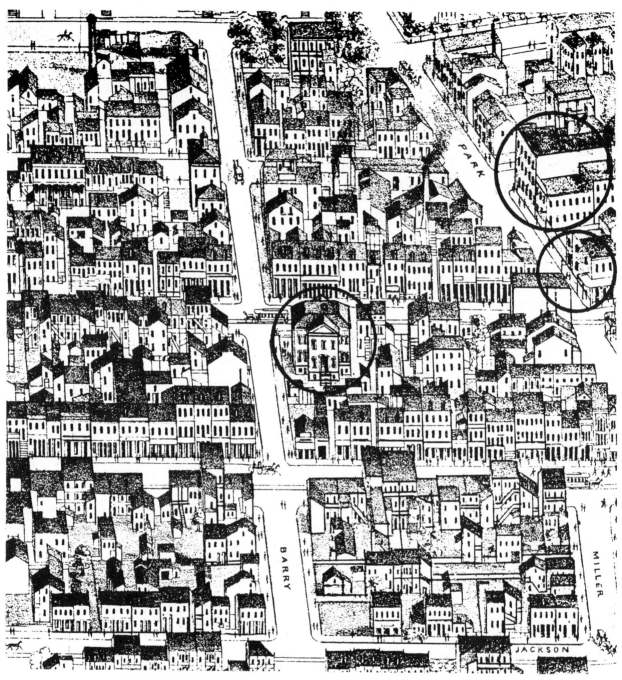

(*Top Right Circle*) Christopher Simpson
Foundry. Located at Eighth and Park.
(*Bottom Right Circle*) Harmonia Hall.
(*Bottom Left Circle*) Pestalozzi School.

Microfilm, Dusty Documents and the Chatter of Little Old Ladies

Newspapers

Newspapers hold the greatest amount of untapped St. Louis source material. There are excellent files available at the Mercantile Library, the Missouri Historical Society at Jefferson Memorial, and at the St. Louis City Library. The best place to work is at the Mercantile. Miss Mary Mewes, Research Librarian, is most cooperative. Bound volumes of the original newspapers are provided to the researcher, thus making work go faster and be much more enjoyable. For this project, over three decades of daily papers were read and searched for information. Among the files consulted were: the *Free Press*, the *Missouri Democrat*, the *Missouri Republican*, the *Saint Louis Daily Globe*, the *Saint Louis Daily Union*, the *Saint Louis Globe-Democrat*, the *Saint Louis Luminary* (a source of rare humor), the *Saint Louis Post-Dispatch*, the *Saint Louis Texan*, the *Saint Louis Times*, the *Saint Louis Star Times*, and the *Weekly Pilot*.

Oral Histories and Helpers

Many older citizens of St. Louis were consulted, and three proved to be particularly helpful. Julia Davis is a veritable storehouse of information about Saint Louis Negro history. She was most generous in sharing her knowledge. Mrs. Gordon Pullis Henderson gave valuable information about the Pullis family. Genevieve Pullis proved to be the greatest treasure of all. Her knowledge of the city, and in particular Frenchtown, is phenomenal. The wit and sense of humor with which she embellishes her conversation make consulting her a most enjoyable experience. I will never forget her first comment, "John, I've led a very seamy life." With such an opening who could resist giving her their undivided attention. Louis F. Heger, born in the area in 1894, recited descriptions of the blocks, building by building.

Cemeteries

Bellefontaine and Calvary Cemeteries are excellently equipped to handle researchers. Their records are complete and usually accurate. Unfortunately, poor Arend Rutgers was found to have been listed for over a century as a woman, and his name misspelled as Arena. Getting information from the Old Cathedral records concerning burials, births, etc., is an entirely different matter. The method employed there is to delay and hope you forget to come back. Repeated visits are of little avail.

City Records

The Probate and Circuit Court Records are carefully indexed, easy to use, and were of great assistance in tracing the Clamorgan and Rutgers families. The Saint Louis Marriage Records are also readily available. The Recorder of Deeds Office is an abysmal mess! There you are met with little cooperation, and everyone pretends complete ignorance (Let's hope it is pretense). The indexes are among the worst in the nation. If it were not for the records of the private title companies, Saint Louis real estate sales would grind to a halt.

City Directories

The various city directories proved to be a good source for supplying addresses and such information as business partnerships, approximate dates of death, etc. Directories are available at the various libraries and date from 1821 to the present. They include: *Paxton's Directory, Charles Keemle's St. Louis Directory, Green's St. Louis Directory, J. H. Sloss' St. Louis Directory, R. V. Kennedy's St. Louis Directory, Edward's Directory, Gould's Directory, Gould's St. Louis Blue Book* (listing only the elite, but arranged by address as well as by name).

U.S. Census Reports

The U.S. Census Reports for 1850, 1860, 1870,

and 1880 were carefully studied, and they yielded rich rewards. The Slave and Mortality Schedules were also consulted. Clarification of family relationships, occupations, ages, amounts of wealth, places of birth, and the tendency of some to prevaricate--all become apparent as one reads the Census. Fascinating bits of information are revealed, such as the individual who died of "toe itch," having suffered for thirteen days. The census records for the nation are available at the St. Louis City Library.

Manuscript Collections

The Missouri Historical Society, located in the Jefferson Memorial Building in St. Louis, has an excellent manuscript collection. Among the collections consulted and used in the writing of *Frenchtown* were: the Case Family Papers, the Chouteau Collection, James S. Copley's Civil War Papers (the originals are in La Jolla, California), the Delany Papers, the Hamilton R. Gamble Papers, the Green Papers, the James Harrison Collection, the Land Papers, the William Carr Lane Collection, the George E. Leighton Collection, the Lucas Papers, the William M. McPheeters Collection, the P. Chouteau Maffitt Collection, the Mullanphy Family Papers, the Stella Olshausen Papers, the Peugnet Collection, the John G. Priest Collection, the St. Stephen's Episcopal Church Records (1886-1917), Dr. William G. Swekosky's letters and "St. Louis Buildings File," the George R. Taylor Collection, the Dexter Tiffany Collection (particularly valuable for information on Free Negroes of St. Louis).

Excellent research materials are available in the Swekosky Collection at Notre Dame College. The collection is massive and consists of thousands of photographs of vanished St. Louis architecture, as well as abstract material concerning the various owners of the structures. Admission is by appointment.

The libraries of the St. Louis Medical Society and of the Medical School of Washington University hold much material treating Dr. Joseph Nash McDowell. The latter has the various catalogues of McDowell's College.

Special Friends

Several people offered assistance with this project, but foremost among them were Emory Hampel and E. Robert Eastin. Emory, a language teacher at Webster Groves High School, translated E. D. Kargau's late-nineteenth-century description of St. Louis (the original is in German). For Emory it was a labor of love. For me it proved to be of immense help in getting the proper feel for the old German neighborhoods of Frenchtown. It is hoped that Emory's translation will be someday published.

E. Robert Eastin took an early interest in this project and was a frequent companion on research ventures. He had hoped to write the chapter which treats his relatives, the Olshausens, but various emergencies prevented him from doing so.

Marilynne Bradley took many of the pictures included in the work. Her talent as an artist is vividly displayed in several drawings which she did from very faded photographs.

Books and Articles

A Complete List of Exempts in St. Louis Division E.M.M. St. Louis, 1862.

A List of Disloyal and Disfranchised Persons in St. Louis County. St. Louis, 1866.

Anderson, Galusha. *A Border City During The Civil War.* Boston, 1908.

Baldwin, Helen I., and others. *Heritage of St. Louis.* St. Louis, 1964.

Baptismal Record Book #2 of St. Vincent de Paul Church, 1844-1851. St. Vincent de Paul Church, St. Louis, Missouri.

Beale, Howard K., ed. "The Diary of Edward Bates," *Annual Report of the American Historical Association.* 4 vols. Washington, D. C., 1933.

Bennett, Elliott C. *Index: St. Louis City Ordinances 1822-1903.*

Billon, Clara. Journal, 1890's. Billon Collection. Missouri Historical Society, St. Louis, Missouri.

Billon, Frederick L. *Annals of St. Louis in its Territorial Days From 1804 to 1821.* St. Louis, 1888.

Boyer, Mary Joan. *The Old Gravois Coal Diggings.* Cape Girardeau, 1968.

Brodman, Estelle. "Joseph Nash McDowell, The Great Eccentric." Read at Friends of the Kornhauser Health Sciences Library, University of Louisville, Kentucky, April 5, 1976.

Bryan, John Albury, ed. *Missouri's Contribution to American Architecture.* St. Louis, 1928.

Bulger, Harold A. "Early Years of the Missouri Medical College," *The Washington University Medical Alumni Quarterly*, II (July, 1939).

Bush, Isidor. "The Jews of St. Louis," *Bulletin of the Missouri Historical Society*, VIII (October, 1951).

Campbell, R. A., ed. *Campbell's Gazeteer of Missouri*. 1875.

Carson, William G. B. "Secesh," *Bulletin of the Missouri Historical Society*, XXIII (January, 1967).

Checkerlinks: 60th Anniversary Edition. St. Louis (January-February, 1954).

"Children of Lebanon in St. Louis," St. Louis *Republic*, March 29, 1903.

"Chouteau Avenue: A Meditation (c. 1916)," *Bulletin of the Missouri Historical Society*, VI (January, 1950).

Christensen, Lawrence O. "Cyprian Clamorgan, The Colored Aristocracy of St. Louis (1858)," *Bulletin of the Missouri Historical Society*, XXXI (October, 1974).

Church of St. Vincent de Paul Centennial Jubilee. St. Louis, 1944.

"The City of St. Louis," *The Atlantic Monthly*, XIX (June, 1867).

Cleland, B. *A Historical Account of All the Mayors, Since the Formation of the City Government of St. Louis to the Present Date--1846*, and

Some Odes. St. Louis, 1846.

Clemens, Helen. Scrapbook, 1861. Scrapbook File. Missouri Historical Society, St. Louis, Missouri.

Collet, *Oscar W. Collet's St. Louis Archives 1804-1854*. Grantors, I N-Z. 1874.

Commercial and Architectural St. Louis. St. Louis, 1888.

Compton, Richard J., and Camille N. Dry. *Pictorial St. Louis: A Topographical Survey*. St. Louis, 1875.

Cox, James. *Old and New St. Louis: A Concise History of the Metropolis of the West and Southwest, With a Review of its Present Greatness and Immediate Prospects*. 2 vols. St. Louis, 1894.

Crinklaw, Don. "The Lemps of St. Louis," St. Louis *Post-Dispatch*, December 2, 1973.

Cunningham, Mary B., and Jeanne C. Blythe. *The Founding Family of St. Louis*. St. Louis, 1977.

Dalton, Mary Louise. "Notes on the Genealogy of the Vallé Family," *Missouri Historical Society*, II (October, 1906).

Darby, John F. *Personal Recollections of John F. Darby*. St. Louis, 1880.

Davis, Julia. *Calendar of Information Series From*

September 1, 1966 to August 31, 1967, For Banneker District Pupils.

Day, Judy, and M. James Kedro. "Free Blacks in St. Louis: Antebellum Conditions, Emancipation, and the Postwar Era," *Bulletin of the Missouri Historical Society, XXX* (January, 1974).

Dick, Everett. *The Dixie Frontier: A Comprehensive Picture of Southern Frontier Life Before the Civil War.* New York, 1948.

Edwards, Edward. *History of the Volunteer Fire Department of St. Louis.* St. Louis, 1906.

Edwards, Richard. *Edward's Great West and Her Commercial Metropolis.*

Essex, James Cartwright. "Excerpts From an Autobiography (1811-1890)," *Glimpses of the Past*, I, Missouri Historical Society, I (June, 1934).

Frost, Griffin. *Camp and Prison Journal.* Quincy, Illinois, 1867.

Garesche, Louis J. *Biography of Lieut. Col. Julius P. Garesche.* Philadelphia, 1887.

Gill, McCune. *The St. Louis Story.* 3 vols. St. Louis, 1952.
——————*The Streets of St. Louis.* St. Louis, 1920.

Gould, D. B. *St. Louis Illustrated.*

Grisham, Marjorie E. Fox. "Joseph Nash McDowell and the Medical Department of Kemper College, 1840-45," *Bulletin of the Missouri Historical Society*, XII (July, 1956).

Hardaway, Harriet Lane Cates. "The Adventures of General Frost and His Wife Lily During the Civil War," *Florissant Valley Historical Quarterly*, XIV (July, 1972).

——————, and Dorothy G. Holland, eds. *Philippine Duchesne and Her Times.* St. Louis, 1968.

Hofacker, Erich P. *German Literature As Reflected in the German-Language Press of St. Louis Prior to 1898.* St. Louis, 1946.

Hogan, Honest John. *Thoughts About the City of St. Louis: Her Commerce and Manufactures, Railroads, Etc.* St. Louis, 1854.

Holland, Dorothy Garesche. *The Garesche, De Bauduy and Des Chapelles Families: History and Genealogy.* St. Louis, 1963.

Hunicke Family Chart. Stella Olshausen Papers, owned by Mrs. Elizabeth Cullinane, Ladue, Missouri.

Hutawa, Julius. *Map of the City of St. Louis.* St. Louis, 1852.

Hyde, William. *Newspapers & Newspaper People of Three Decades.* St. Louis, 1896.

——————, and Howard L. Conrad, eds. *Encyclopedia of the History of St. Louis: A Compendium of History and Biography For Ready Reference*, 4 vols. St. Louis, 1899.

Isaacs, Deborah. "Antebellum Days in St. Louis," St. Louis *Republic*, March 29, 1903.

——————"Confederate Days in St. Louis," St. Louis *Republic*, May 3, 1903.

Jensen, Dana O. "The Enigma of Mr. Shaw," *Bulletin of the Missouri Historical Society*, XV (July, 1959).

Jones, Pat. "What Ever Happened to Bohemian Hill?" Unpublished manuscript written for graduate seminar at U.M.S.L in 1974.

125th Jubilee of St. John Nepomuk Church: First Czech Catholic Church in America. St. Louis, 1979.

Kargau, E.D. *Mercantile, Industrial and Professional St. Louis.* St. Louis, 1902 or 1903.

Kelsoe, W. A. *St. Louis Reference Record: A Newspaper Man's Motion-Picture of the City When We Got Our First Bridge, and of Many Later Happenings of Local Note.* St. Louis, 1928.

Kennerly, James. Diary (February 18, 1926-November 19, 1838). Missouri Historical Society, St. Louis, Missouri.

Kennerly, William Clark. *Persimmon Hill: A Narrative of Old St. Louis and the Far West.* Norman, Oklahoma, 1948.

Lane, William Carr. "Letters of William Carr Lane (1819-1831)," *Glimpses of the Past*, VII, Missouri Historical Society, VII (July-September, 1940).

Leftwich, Rev. W. M. *Martyrdom in Missouri.* 2 vols. St. Louis, 1870.

Leonard, John W. ed. *The Book of St. Louisans: A Biographical Dictionary of Leading Living Men of the City of St. Louis.* St. Louis, 1906.

——————*Industries of St. Louis: Her Relations As a Center of Trade.* St. Louis, 1887.

"The Maronites in St. Louis," St. Louis *Globe-Democrat*, February 4, 1900.

McDonald, Gen. John. *Secrets of the Great Whiskey Ring.* Chicago, 1880.

Mook, George J. Civil War Diary (begins January 1, 1865). George J. Mook Collection. Missouri Historical Society, St. Louis, Missouri.

Morrison, Adele Sarpy. *Memoirs of Adele Sarpy Morrison.* St. Louis, 1911.

Nasatir, A. P. "Jacques Clamorgan: Colonial Promoter of the Northern Border of New Spain," *New Mexico Historical Review*, XVII (April, 1942).

Negroes: Their Gift to St. Louis. St. Louis, 1964.

Orthwein, Walter E. "Protestants Outlawed by Spain: 11 Baptists Built First Church Here in 1818," St. Louis *Globe Democrat*, March 1, 1964.

Parkin, Robert E. "Earliest Registers of the First Catholic Church of St. Louis," *St. Louis*

Genealogical Society Quarterly, III (June, 1970).

Pen & Sunlight Sketches of St. Louis: The Commercial Gateway to the South. Chicago, c. 1891.

Platbook of St. Louis, 1880's. Missouri Historical Society, St. Louis, Missouri.

Real Estate Owners of St. Louis As Shown by the Assessment. St. Louis, 1906.

Reavis, L. U. *St. Louis, The Commercial Metropolis of the Mississippi Valley.* St. Louis, 1874.

"Reminiscences of the Oldest Hearse Driver in St. Louis," St. Louis *Republic*, March 22, 1903.

Rutgers, Arend. Diary (1787-1827). Arthur Garesché Francis Collection. Missouri Historical Society, St. Louis, Missouri.

Scharf, J. Thomas. *History of St. Louis City & & County from the Earliest Period to the Present Day.* 2 vols. Philadelphia, 1883.

Shalhool, George Nassir. "Maronites of St. Louis," *Lebanese American Journal*, May 16, 1960.

Shinkle, Florence. "Wasteland Area in the City," St. Louis *Post-Dispatch*, July 14, 1974.

Shoemaker, Floyd Calvin. *Missouri & Missourians: Land of Contrasts and People of Achievement.* 5 vols. Chicago, 1943.

Skellman, W. D. *The Western Metropolis; or St. Louis in 1846.* St. Louis, 1846.

St. Louis Medical Society Centennial Volume. St. Louis, 1939.

Standish, Myles. "St. Louis Residents Have Maintained Strong Interest in Theater Since 1815," St. Louis *Post-Dispatch*, February 16, 1964.

Stevens, Walter B. *St. Louis: History of the Fourth City (1763-1909).* 3 vols. St. Louis, 1911.

Taylor, Philip. A Brief History of the Public Markets in the City of St. Louis, Missouri. (1961). Reference Room, St. Louis City Library.

Terry, Robert J. "Recalling a Famous Pupil of McDowell's Medical College, Harriet Goodhue Hosmer, Sculptor," *Washington University Medical Alumni Quarterly*, VII (October, 1943).

Thomas, James S. Scrapbook, 1869. Reference Room, Mercantile Library, St. Louis, Missouri.

Thomas, William L. *History of St. Louis County, Missouri.* 2 vols. St. Louis, 1911.

Toft, Carolyn Hewes, ed. *Soulard: The Ethnic Heritage of an Urban Neighborhood.* St. Louis, 1975.

"1896 Tornado," *St. Louis Genealogical Society Quarterly*, VIII (June, 1975).

Van Nada, M. L. ed. *The Book of Missourians.* St. Louis, 1906.

Van Ravensway, Charles. "Anna Maria von Phul,"

Bulletin of the Missouri Historical Society, (April, 1954).

Vexler, Robert. ed. *St. Louis: A Chronological & Documentary History.* Dobbs Ferry, N. Y., 1974.

Whipple's Daily Fire Reporter. St. Louis, 1882.

Wilks, Ed. "The Unsolved Murder of Barbara Jean," St. Louis *Post-Dispatch*, February 25, 1973.

Williams, Henry W. *History, Abstracts of Title, Evidences of Location, Etc. Relating to the Common Field lots of the South Grand Prairie and Cul de Sac of the Grand Prairie, and an Argument in Support of Cozens' Surveys.* St. Louis, 1854.

The Whole Story Told: The Dark & Mysterious Places of St. Louis. St. Louis, 1885.